# *Maki*

## Biography of a Natural Medium

Hilary Harcourt

# DEDICATION
## Phyllis Albutt

*To my family in the trust they will understand, and with love and thanks to the many friends who embody my greater family in this life.*

The names of characters in this book have been changed, apart from Phyllis Albutt and the late Mrs. Charge, who remain genuine through and through.

# CONTENTS

*Making Angels*

*"Everyone who is seriously engaged in the pursuit of science becomes convinced that the laws of nature manifest the existence of a spirit vastly superior to that of men."*

(Einstein; Letter of 24 January 1936 to a schoolgirl, Phyllis Wright)

*Making Angels*

# ACKNOWLEDGMENTS

There are always a myriad unsung heroes standing behind an author and the question that hangs heaviest in the air is not who to include, but who to leave out. Seems impossible to choose when it's never just about who was there when you actually wrote the book, but who led you to that point. In that case, for me, it starts a long time ago - the teacher who told me that 99% of his English students had technical ability, but only 1% had flair (and that was me). I was 15. Admittedly, this suggests my grammatical ability was duff; nonetheless, I rehearsed this before I enrolled for my first degree and when I found this manuscript and a thousand times in between. That teacher was Mr. Tyson and I never thanked him before he died. I have felt that burden of omission throughout my life, so I'm releasing it here. Next came Deborah Greenup who worked for a publishing company and read a pretty awful first book from her hospital bed and gave me invaluable, genuinely kind, encouragement. I was 21. I shall never forget you either. Where next and where to end? These thoughts have taken me to all kinds of people and impossible choices, where I battled with love, duty, indebtedness. I love that I got to be so many things to so many people, yet the answer to how I should order the souls that have 'made' my life as a writer, eludes me. What I do know is that I must resist the desire to write a book of acknowledgements and concentrate on those who directly contributed to this book. Here are those souls:

Phyllis for her wonderful life, husband Colin, for keeping things going when my mind was elsewhere, son Greg, brothers Rob and Chris for support, Cousin Keith for editing advice, the 'Forest locals', particularly Nessie, Hannah and Michelle for encouragement (yoga and wine) and writing the 'About the Author' blurb. Special thanks to 'Chris Bluett Photography' for the front cover. Finally, a 'thank you' to my Dudley family and all my friends behind the scenes – 'you', at least know who you are, as do those who left me their hearts too soon to show me the way. *I'll be seeing you…*

# PREFACE

*"Life can only be understood backwards; but it must be lived forwards."* (Kierkegaard)

I've been sitting here trying to remember when I first saw her? This normal, everyday, housewife with the soft eyes; gentle, green eyes that can, quite inexplicably, fill with mist when she speaks to you. You wonder if it's a good thing or not? You wonder, if there's an insight that's clouded her vision for a moment, or whether she's just concentrating and forgetting to blink like people do? Then, all too quickly, before you've answered your own questions, those eyes are upon you and you are aware that something passed between you. Of course, you don't know what.

Still held in this gaze, you fail to be perturbed by its gentle introspection; content instead to ponder upon the way of things, as quite beyond the life between you. Too soon, the moment has passed and you recognise yourself in those eyes – they are full of everyday clutter, the shopping lists, lunch boxes and the ceaseless timetable of motherhood itself. Finally… yes, finally… she speaks to you in a stilted, thoughtful way and you listen, and still you're not sure why this is so very important.

It is about this time that a serenity washes away the mundane and the ordinary to leave a blank page onto which she invites you to write your troubles and your heartfelt desires. I am wondering who listens to her worries. She must have them, because gentleness is not borne of an unmeasured life, nor unfaltering confidence in self. No, the empathy she has, in the arms of any logic, will not find such peace as this.

I imagine her serenity is tinged with loneliness. How can it not be? Who wouldn't be lonely when you can look into another's face and sometimes see their past and sometimes their future; who wouldn't be lonely with these thoughts? I've watched her work – saw the nods, denial followed by recognition, diminishing puzzlement, the blushes, the tears, the thanks.

At these times, she feels life's full force, she is buoyant, enjoying being at the helm with the sun in her face. She is briefly sharing the chapters of the life she is reading, but the whole book she can never read. I don't even think she understands what she's reading and she has to turn the page far too quickly. It is a lost kingdom she inhabits; lost and lonely. Or so it seemed to me then.

So here I sit, trying to picture her years later and I'm suddenly quite aware of the thoughts of some readers, simply because they were once my own – how is it possible to read another's life story, to 'know' another's character, hopes and dreams, without even a cursory introduction? I don't have an answer that would satisfy everyone, even though, over time, I turned my brain into knots contemplating this very question. I don't think it's possible given what we know, or don't know now, and I stopped asking at the point I had seen enough of her mediumship to just accept her gift – a gift that hijacked her life and from which she never profited. For these reasons, I accept it with the same knowingness that light alters dark and snow is a myriad, dazzling particles, sunshine makes me happy, and I wrote the first draft when I was 33 and I'm now 65.

Why did it take that long? Mostly because life took over and we walked in different directions, in more ways than one: I went to the most southerly point of the UK, Phyllis stayed in the Midlands. This parting of ways was also philosophical. I went to work in academia, a place where proof of life after death is not possible and so the concept of spirit consciousness is a non-starter. This is simply because our own consciousness is viewed as arising from the physical brain's mechanics and nothing more – no brain, no mind, no consciousness, no spirit. It follows that awareness of 'spirit people' is either a matter of oxygen deficiency or delusion. So I found answers, but not the ones I wanted. I think we have to look with better eyes than logical inference affords us.

Fortunately, I then retired from academia, and had cataract surgery when I moved to the Forest of Dean in 2020 and so, when I came across the draft manuscript in a packing crate, I was seeing more clearly in every way. As I researched American Indian philosophy for the book – for reasons that will become clear – I came across a Sioux text. It said, *'the longest journey we can make in this life is from the head to the heart'*. It seemed to be talking to me – I had got 'out of my head' and had reached my heart at last. I was ready to write, except that now, I couldn't find Phyllis.

Phyllis was no longer living in Droitwich. She seemed to have disappeared off the face of this world; not even the inescapable social media footprint found her. Yet, when the time was right (and as elastic, expendable and esoteric as that evidently is to the spirit world), I found her son on Face Book and then tracked her down in the rolling countryside of Wales. She is now 77.

One day I will tell you this story but, for now, I just want to tell you hers.

# CHAPTER 1

**Grace is not something we're born with**

*"The two most important days of your life are the day you're born and the day that you find out why."*
(Mark Twain)

On 11 July 1945, Grace Hughes gave birth to a normal, blotchy red, seemingly unlaundered, baby girl. Grace had not planned on this child. Her career had already been interrupted twice since her marriage at 29, and it seemed as though fate had, yet again, cast a fickle hand across her path to dash her promising nursing career into the land of the banal, into motherhood yet again.

Throughout pregnancy, the turmoil in 'wishing away' the child was nothing compared to the ironic pain of guilt she felt just two days after birth, as she listened to the doctor:

"I'm sorry Mrs. Hughes, but she is a very sick baby indeed …" The doctor paused to give Grace time to anticipate what might be coming next. "I think tonight will tell us everything we need to know, but…."

He paused again, surveying her, wondering if she were listening; it didn't seem like it. Yet Grace had understood. At 36, she had become a knowledgeable nurse and she had been on her way to Matron… until now. On a professional level then, Grace's conscious mind told her that, in this year of 1945, severe gastroenteritis in a two-day old infant was fatal. On a personal level, her sub-conscience told her that wishing away the child throughout pregnancy was killing her daughter now.

She met the doctor's eyes, all the strength of her personality – and she was strong this one – refused to flinch beneath his stare; the stare that seemed to Grace to accuse her with the impending death of her own child. The doctor finished his sentence at this point, but it disappeared into the ether. Did he know? Could he guess what she was feeling? Did he sense her guilt?

Grace turned away from the doctor and turned to the only person she would entrust the 'inner Grace' to, her God, and so, later that day, she walked down the quiet aisle of her church; the memories of her strong religious upbringing brought her the resolve she needed. It always had. From chorister to Sunday school teacher, it was the living crutch; the only one that had never been kicked away from her. Hadn't it seen her through her own mother's death at 14? And even when her strict father had given up on her and passed her on to Auntie May, hadn't it seen her through then too?

*'God never let you down, people did.'*

That day, as all days that had gone before, the solitude of the church allowed her to be weak, whereas life had always seemed to demand of her strength and, sometimes, just sometimes, that strength would turn to hardness. A hardness that would direct itself at her family (nowhere else) and she didn't really want to know why, because it would mean examining her childhood beyond looking after the little ones, birthday cake, cookery lessons, and earache and, worse still, recognising that her life as a mother had been preordained – it was the role of woman in her 1940s world.

No, she preferred to reflect on the social Grace, the neighbour and friend. This Grace was sturdy, dependable and kind. Throughout the war years, no one feared to knock on her door with their ailments, or their sick children, because she would take charge immediately and give them the care, the certainty, they craved. Had you asked neighbours about Grace, they would have said, 'Oh, Mrs. Hughes, she nurses people'.

Grace, the nurse, was professional, Grace, the wife, dominant, Grace, the mother, indomitable. At times, it felt as though her own children, her own husband, were just life's stumbling blocks, just as her own mother had been. Her mother's death had put the brakes on her chosen career, a career she loved and that loved her… and they'd said, 'someone has to look after her'.

Warm knees touched the stone floor of the front pew. In turn, the hardness of stone touched her, said something to her, she half listened. Her heart became soft by default. She turned her gaze to the heavens and laid her pledge at her God's feet:

"Father, if you will allow me to keep the child, I will give her back to you as a teacher."

These words seem strange to us, but they were not strange to the soul for whom they were spoken, because she did become a teacher, of sorts. We can only speculate that Grace missed the sign of acquiescence here as, for her, the air was still heavy with silence, as if even he were surprised by the bargain they had just struck for the child called Phyllis.

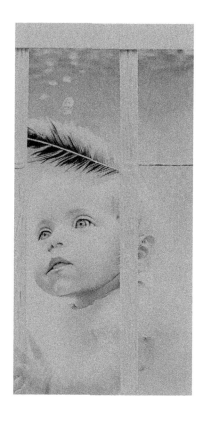

# CHAPTER 2

### A Fish Out of Water

*"Everybody is a genius, but if you judge a fish by its ability to climb a tree, it will live its whole life believing that it is stupid."* (Einstein)

I was born in a two-up, two-down, back-to-back, terrace in the centre of Birmingham. We had a small sitting room and an even smaller kitchen. We had gas lights on the wall, but electricity wasn't long in coming. I had a sister called Sophie and a brother, Patrick. My mother was strong and my father, soft. But long before I knew these simple facts, I was aware of being an individual, quite apart from these people, whom I would come to love nonetheless, each in a different way.

I remember, so very clearly (crystal clear), lying in my cot (glass-bottom boat, in my imagination), seeing baby fingers in my horizontal line of vision (they were mine), sensing the imprisonment; testing, with small curling finger tips, the rigid bars of the boat's bow. Bobbing around on a sea of possibilities, I look around the sitting room to see different sorts of people. These would be my mother, my father and my brother and sister. Although, as I gaze, I am unaware of their relationship to me, I do know – with a clarity of vision that is beyond my age – that these people will care for me, though I shall never quite 'belong' to them.

I watch as a strong looking woman organises her children. The man is in the shadows. It seems to me to be a very solemn business I'm witnessing. The little girl has brown, wispy, shoulder-length hair. A serious child this one, who would carry a book in her hand. Then there is the little boy, he would carry a bat in his hand, but for now, he is respectfully listening to the woman. I sense that, although he isn't smiling, a smile would never be far away. The boy was like an open book I could peer into. I liked this being. I knew he would pull faces at me, but never behind me; an honest, open-faced, dark haired child, different to the girl.

I am knowing this because I am connected to another being. I am listening carefully. I understand words in my head, although I have no spoken language yet. It never occurs to me that I shouldn't be able to understand what is happening. I will come to liken it to listening to a radio – in the beginning, you don't know where the sound is coming from, you don't even know the sound is a language – all you do know is that you understand the message and, by the time you do understand it all, it's irrelevant, there's just the 'ghost in the machine'. And that's real. I'm quite happy with these strange thoughts, so I stop wondering, even though I am unaware that I am wondering, and allow my boat to sail into sleep, as it frequently did.

Another day, another clear day, and I'm peering into the coal fire. This is a remarkable source of magic to me – a point of concentration, when I would think about nothing in particular, just see pictures. On this day, I see numbers and letters arranged in a semi-circle. It is a Ouija board – I don't know it's called this, I just know I don't like it. It is not for me.

No other thoughts stayed with me so completely, until about four or five years of age. At this time, I was sharing a bed with my sister, Sophie. My brother, Patrick, shared our room too and so we were all together, all secure, all happy. I'm guessing this is the very reason I remained at peace when I became aware of a hand touching mine; a slow realisation of a strange, disembodied man's hand in mine, which held no fear for me at all, because it belonged to the being I had sensed so many times before.

I fell asleep then and into dream, into a peaceful new land where I viewed wonders yet to be experienced by me (or by anyone else at that time). The things I remember vividly were V-shaped wings on aircraft, which looked like paper darts (they were delta wings first seen on the F-102 in October 1953). I saw boats skimming the surface of water (hovercrafts, c.1955); a big pool surrounded by palm trees and, above my head, the sky took the form of a transparent dome. (I recognised Center Parcs from a picture I saw when they first appeared in 1987).

There were more 'revelations', but the most vivid and recurring, was when my friend (the owner of the gentle hand) led me into a forest clearing and, while he made a fire, he would tell me all manner of stories. I was enthralled, always sitting intently and contentedly with him, as he fed the flames of the campfire and my imagination. I had no fear, just peacefulness; the sort you have when you're with someone you love and trust implicitly. Everything I experienced at these peaceful times though was purposeful – this *being* was refining my senses, honing my observations, teaching me focus. Everything contained a lesson, whether I knew it or not.

It was during one of these fireside chats that I was told something that was to happen much later – I would be with this family until I was 21 years of age and then I would leave. I came to believe this was something everyone did; a sort of rite of passage for 21-year olds.

Despite my friend's almost everyday presence, I couldn't have described him to anyone at that time, although I knew instinctively that the presence was male. This dilemma of *who, what, why* and *when* didn't seem to be one then. I suppose because, as a child, I accepted many things in an innocent and pure way.

I can't even remember all the stories he told me, but, in later years, stories that seemed to come from nowhere, off 'the top of my head', would captivate friends' attention. I was good at telling stories and I knew it. Having said that, I was not telling stories when, on arriving home from junior school one Wednesday afternoon, I made a pronouncement to Mother:

"We're going to stay with Auntie for the weekend," I said.

Mother looked at me and I like to think it was a 'weird child, good job I love you' moment I saw flitting across her face. Wishful thinking though it may well have been, she certainly didn't know anything about this plan, yet there were no recriminations from her. I don't know how I knew about the impending trip, but it was absolute knowledge. I hadn't heard it, seen a vision, anything glorious, just another crystal clear, glass-bottom boat, certainty.

Auntie called Mother next day to invite us children to spend the weekend at the farm. We loved the freedom there.

This wasn't an isolated incident – there were many such pronouncements made over the years – and I was very fortunate in that Mother never seemed to be that fazed by my predictions. I wasn't to know that she had started visiting Spiritualist meetings when she was 30 years old until much later and it struck me as odd, as she was from such a conventional church-going background. It never occurred to me to ask her why she had started going, or whether she had abilities too.

Her interest in Spiritualism was fortunate for me though, because it gave her the awareness that there was mystery in the world and this allowed me to be just what I was, free of recriminations and free of the legacy of superstition, and free to play my favourite game:

"Mother, are you thinking about … so-and-so?" I would ask. (The *so-and-so* could be a colour, person, event, or even just a feeling).

I wasn't always right in this 'mind game', but 'frequently so' would be a fair assessment. Mother would simply answer with a 'yes' or a 'no'. I don't know if she were trying to encourage me or not but, at the time, I just felt at liberty to experiment. In hindsight, that was some gift she gave me.

Although these games were a source of great pleasure to me, the happiest times of my childhood were always those hours I spent alone in my (well, *our*) bedroom. I can especially recall looking at pictures of the stars and planets and, while I was not able to pronounce the names of them (or read for that matter), they transported me out of this reality into another dimension and, to me, a real place.

These pictures would allow my mind to reach out into the very space they depicted. A mind, set free of limitation, could fly unbounded by space-time; the reality we know as physical life. Here, I became pure consciousness, beginning to sense, touch and experience a far greater awareness. These days, it's fashionable to call this state an energy field, quantum space, magical portal, or vortex – we're all trying to fill the longing we have for a state of grace beyond intellect. A place where we can glimpse our essence, our source and find 'home'. You might as well call a black hole 'Doris', it just doesn't do it justice.

Staring at pictures of flying fish on my bedroom wall was another personal favourite pastime of mine, as a way of unleashing my mind. Perhaps it was the thought of fish doing something they weren't supposed to that captivated me – they were breaking the mould, like me. I liked that idea very much and would sit on my bed and fly with them. I wondered later if this were where Einstein got his idea about fish and intellect from. I like to think he did and had a flying fish obsession in childhood like me.

Yes, I liked that idea very much, especially as school wasn't for me. It was, possibly, my need for peace and freedom (not to mention a strong personality, compliments of my mother) that had created total rebellion against school life. School epitomised the authoritative process that took away freedom. It invalidated the intuitive mind; that part of you that school dare not encourage, in case it incited rebellion.

It seemed absolutely clear to me that teachers wanted to strangle intuition and bring it subservient to the God of logic, of repetition, method, cause and effect – and I would have none of it! I fought with a strength of will that was inherent in me.

I don't know where it came from, but it was as if I were fighting for my very life. I think I was really fighting for my right to be different and that meant the right to retain an intuitively, predictive mind. After all, if you cover one eye for several years, gradually you lose the use of that eye. So it is with the intuitive mind, you have to let it fly like a fish out of water and never believe that you are stupid.

# CHAPTER 3

## Cross My Heart and Hope to Die

*"Fortunately, some are born with spiritual immune systems that … begin sensing that something is amiss, and start looking for answers… so begins the journey of awakening."*
(Henri Bergson)

At 9 years of age, I was given some insight into Mother's 'other life' as a person separate from me, as well as something of her plans for me. One Thursday afternoon, she took me to a Spiritualist meeting with her. Spiritualism was still very much an exclusive club then (there were no Mediums on the Internet, or psychic readings popping up in your in-box). I remember how exciting it was to be in a secret society. It was to be Enid Blyton's 'Secret Seven'

Society's most covert mission – we couldn't tell anyone we were going and certainly not what happened there.

We walked up a back stair to the meeting at the back of an echoey, stone, municipal building. It was cool. I looked down at my sister's cast-off blue dress and school shoes, feeling slightly disappointed that we didn't have to do a secret knock before they let us in. I felt duty-bound though, to take a vow of secrecy in my mind as we crossed the threshold – *'Cross my heart and hope to die'*.

Once in, it didn't seem so very unusual to me. It was a bit of a disappointment actually. Enid Blyton (referred to as 'the Medium' by Mother) seemed to me to be at least 90, but given my age, she was probably in her 40s. She was a well-built woman and her personality was as strong as her bristly, grey hair. I remember her saying a prayer and the little group sang a hymn and then, almost unperceptively, I became aware of the feeling of being generally unwell.

The feeling of disappointment was being replaced with a growing malaise. I couldn't pin it down – couldn't say I felt sick to the stomach, or had a headache, or any other tangible symptom, but still I felt really ill. The feeling grew and, as it did, the energy was draining from my body.

I was very aware of Mother beside me and I knew I mustn't fidget. You didn't do that. Everything was on a knife-edge in my head. Her glance told me I was slouching. I wondered if she were thinking she shouldn't have brought me. 'I had to keep still.'

I sat, hands in lap, unable to do anything about the waves of sickness now washing over me. It felt interminable. Time had screeched to a halt in front of me and a big second hand reached into my belly and squeezed my stomach into a knot.

*'Cross my heart and hope to die.'*

It was some consolation to me that I then noted the Medium's murmurings were directed elsewhere. It was distant and I was anonymous at least. At the very moment this thought registered though, her attention was suddenly on me, although she was looking through me, maybe just to my left … both?

As I pondered this, she said something to me that didn't make the slightest sense:

"I can see many reams of different coloured material around you… you will always handle scissors and work with colour."

I was far too unwell to come to any conclusions about what this might mean, and it was about this time that the Medium's gaze turned to my mother and she said:

"Please don't bring her here until she's old enough to cope with the emotion. She will be a good Medium this one, but *she is not ready…*"

She emphasised the last words as if Mother had become really deaf at that point. If someone had said I was destined to become a teacher of sorts, I would have found that very amusing indeed, but I was. I was to become a *Fisher of Men.*

# CHAPTER 4

## A Child at Arm's Length

*"I have learned silence from the talkative, toleration from*
*the intolerant, and kindness from the unkind; yet, strange,*
*I am ungrateful to those teachers."* (Kahlil Gibran)


At the age of 11, I started my periods, which was early
for girls of my generation. Mother, being a nurse, wasn't
fazed by this, so neither was I. It did seem though, that this
maturation process brought change with it. I had insights –
my mind seemed to be travelling at 100 miles per hour
compared to other children. I realised too that they didn't
speak of the same things, so I knew they weren't sharing my
reality. I also experienced my reality as high speed because
consciousness was coming from outside, bringing with it

such a wealth of technicolour information that it overrode the evidence coming from my own senses about the physical world.

When you don't share experiences with people, you are destined to have a hard time – you don't feel as though you belong and so you struggle to understand why people take the world around them so seriously and why they obey its conventional wisdom so readily. Or at least I did – I simply struggled to take any notice of other ways of being in the world, because I had my own source of guidance and it was immutable.

By contrast, I found the guidance of 'the family' much more questionable and so, by 14, I had turned into a pure observer, becoming even more aware of the individuals in my family – their personalities, their hopes and motivations, and the pecking order.

My father's personality surfaced quietly and gently, hardly breaking water. Whereas, Mother was firmly at the helm – directing, dominating and dishing out the orders. Sophie and Patrick were being tossed about on the foaming breakwater of Mother's dominion and I? I remained strangely apart, watching Mother bringing up my brother and sister – the feeding, the washing, the dressing, but mostly, the irrepressible guidance and I waited for my turn. It was not to come.

I was a child held at arm's length.

Fortunately, this bobbing about without a compass did have its benefits, as in Mother's eyes, an integral part of her care-giving was discipline, and while she was not averse to giving Sophie and Patrick a good belting, I seemed to escape relatively unscathed. It was as if those first knowing thoughts (when I had peered from between the bars of my cot) of not really belonging, were coming true.

Despite the freedom, I couldn't help but wonder why she didn't treat me the same. I later speculated that, in giving me away to her God, she had left my fate to him – maybe you had to be kinder to a 'God-child'? I did wonder if she loved me. I loved her; I loved her for doing the very best she could – a '50's woman thirsting for independence was not a bad person, she just didn't want to be a mother, so she struck out at the people that had ensnared her. Having said that, she *was* meant to be *my* mother, because she guided me towards 'parent spirit' very early on.

Meanwhile, while I was making sense of home life, the guidance of school continued. It seemed endless. I was as disconnected to it, as my mother was to me. I was still unwilling to surrender to its parrot-fashion tutorial and the one-willed dictatorship of one teacher, one thought, one way.

Instead, I was preoccupied with this inner knowledge that flowed from an unseen source; a source that continued to show me things far more interesting than the life around me. I saw the colours of life itself – every colour seemed to have music attached to it and it could carry a message. It seemed clear to me too, that people not only wore colours, but emitted them too.

No wonder I was preoccupied at school, subject to raised eyebrows from teachers, or feeling distant to many of the children around me, as I gazed with wonder at the colours that emanated from their auras. Auras that projected from the top of their heads down to their shoulders. They were usually bright and beautiful, sometimes dark and dingy.

No wonder too, that I viewed school, as a whole, as a dirty grey and thoroughly deserving of my disdain. It meant I blanked out a lot of what happened there. This was particularly so because I felt school simply got in the way of me learning from my spirit friend.

Sometimes, I would feel one of my class mates was in trouble – usually something in their familiar auras would change and alert me – yet I was stopped from saying anything about it by 'my friend'. I 'knew' it was not my place and that annoyed me. The reality was, school was too crowded, too impersonal and there was nowhere to hide once you'd shown your true colours. I'm guessing it was for this reason that I always knew when I was about to be indiscrete about my gift, as I would be shown traffic lights by my special friend – I was taught when to speak and when to be silent. It became natural rule-following behaviour that I stopped questioning in the end. It's something we all do – even if there's no traffic for miles around, we still stop on red. So did I – same rule, just different authority.

Another thing I was taught in my teenage years was to take responsibility for the gift I had been given and to take people as I found them; not to judge them, but to work with what they gave me and to go at their pace, not mine. 'Never reveal more than the person can cope with,' I was told. I was also taught that it was not my role to change anyone, as we are all given time, which we call 'life', in which to do our best. This time was to be occupied as we saw fit – no pressure, or judgment – no sharp whack across the knuckles here – you didn't even have to fill it with other people's needs.

As I learned these basic lessons, my personality was forming stronger and stronger by the term and, with it, came this irrepressible, and potentially nauseating, certainty that 'I was right'. Hardly surprising then, that I decided to leave school at 15. I left with thoughts of working with my hands – I was no wordsmith, and I had no qualifications to speak of, so I had decided upon either becoming a hairdresser, or a seamstress.

I very quickly fell on my feet, finding a job that gave me a skill I was to love. I joined a family business run by 'The Rosenbergs', a delightful Jewish couple. I began working as a junior, doing what all juniors do – making tea, running errands, tidying up. At the same time though, the Rosenbergs made sure I was learning a lot about working with fabric. That, together with self-discipline (a by-product of watching Mother's child rearing), made me into a capable seamstress.

Now the Medium's prediction those years ago about 'different coloured material' and working with scissors and colour was to make perfect sense and that dawned on me slowly one day, when I was allowed to cut a length of plain blue cotton off a reel.

As it happened, this late realisation was a great lesson in mediumship – messages don't always make any sense at the time they are given, but it doesn't mean they're not true. In fact, it's this type of 'delayed' message that often has the greatest impact, despite the fact it's also open to interpretation of 'self-fulfilling prophecy'.

Unfortunately, I learned another lesson while working there. This is confession time, shame time. Obviously, I don't condone prejudice now, but at 15 I did. It came in the form of Raguel, who was the Rosenberg's only, rather indulged, son. Raguel is Hebrew for 'one of the seven archangels' … angel he was not.

Indeed, it is true to say that Raguel had a cruel streak in him; one that enjoyed watching people squirm, particularly junior workers. Despite this, I loved working there and I worked diligently. I loved the other workers too, especially a woman called Ruth, but Raguel's influence, his grimy coloured aura, was always there and I was constantly wondering how he would embarrass, or belittle, me next.

I didn't have to wait long between these episodes usually. This particular day, it had started like any other, travelling on the top floor of the bus and watching all the people's auras fluxing, shifting and blending with others next to them. I found it endlessly fascinating. I was learning what colours meant, how they changed when they met someone else's – they were like melting greeting cards that everyone shared willingly, but no-one ever acted on the information they contained from what I could tell. I was there to watch and learn, but I knew I mustn't say anything to the people that exchanged calling cards in this way. It was private. *The traffic lights were on red.*

Despite nearly missing my stop, I'd arrived in good time. I could have been very late for work, as I had been wondering about a young boy's aura that had startled like starfish dancing on a light tide, when a young girl had to take the only spare seat next to him. It had flushed several times before it settled into the pearliest of pinks and I was still contemplating whether I had witnessed a budding romance when I arrived at work.

As I was early, I had time to admire the new reels of fabric that had arrived first thing that morning; time to sweep the cotton trails from the floor; and then get my assignment for the morning from Mrs. Rosenberg. I was to mark and cut some deep green velvet – 'nap going down' as instructed – ready for the sewing machine. As I worked carefully, I reflected on the fact that every day, or so it seemed, I was being trusted more and more to work with new challenging fabrics. That made me happy.

Later, I was still happy as Ruth and I chatted and she told me about the most recent episode of her neighbour's turbulent love life over our coffee break:

"Thin walls can be a blessing," she concluded with a wink, sipping her coffee to leave her signature red lipstick on the rim of her mug.

I loved her honest acceptance of 'sexually-transmitted life' in the terraced streets; the manner in which she described the noises it emitted in ways that made my imagination sing her praises. It was bawdy and refreshing and, of course, *really* interesting to a 15-year old.

It was looking like a lovely, relaxed day, particularly as I hadn't seen Raguel. So, by lunchtime, when he still hadn't appeared, I was beginning to think my secret wish – for him to fall desperately in love with a woman who insisted they live abroad – had come true. Not so, and as if by magic, Raguel surfaced from his murky depths while we were sitting in the small staff area, eating.  In a heartbeat, I went from happily munching to ghost-white, as Raguel loudly reprimanded me for eating, what he called, 'filth'.

I could barely understand the words issuing from his mouth; they spilled like rotting vegetation over my dainty little sandwich and the piece of porkpie that was airborne, but had yet to reach my mouth. It never did, but the pigeons at the side door were not so easily upset by his words, or by my tears. I threw the morsels while they cooed sympathetically, feeling small in ways I hadn't thought possible and too hungry for justice to eat any more.

I was not to take porkpie ever again as, that day, I was to learn that refusal to eat this meat was central to Jewish identity. Unfortunately, I learned it in a way that taught me to dislike a whole group of people. While I suppose I couldn't blame him for taking me to task, I did take, and still do take, exception to people who choose to vilify the ignorant for their own perverse gratification.

Our relationship just got worse after that. I began to see him as an evil presence. I will never forget the day he told me the Virgin Mary was a prostitute. I looked at this boy-man, boss-man, bully-boy with bewilderment and struggled with the intense shock peculiar to a (now) 16-year old. As always, I could feel that he enjoyed my discomfort – he reveled in my disbelief – and the strength of horror I felt at these times stayed with me whenever I met a Jewish person for several years after that.

No matter what I thought I'd learned so far – or how much spiritual knowledge had been imparted – once I had recovered, my strong personality allowed me to be angry and contemptuous again and I couldn't forgive him and, as Raguel was Jewish, I couldn't forgive 'them' either. A stupid state of defiance, no doubt peculiar to a 16-year old brain chemistry, given that I was, and will always be, grateful to Mamma and Papa Rosenberg. They were a guiding force in my life; one that enabled me to work with the colours I love so much and, ultimately, one that led me to own a small curtain business and support myself.

However, no matter how kind they were, how well they taught me and how inspiring they were, that gratitude was not to stop my anger and, even after I'd left the Rosenbergs three years later, I'm so very sorry to admit, I was still asking people, 'are you a Jew?'

As for Raguel? I don't know if he ever did find the overseas love of his life. I suspect not – too adventurous for Raguel, who was a coward at heart. What I do know for sure is that there was no evil here, just a boy hungering for a self that was worth having.

As for me, compassion grew, not with the passage of time and a developing brain alone – and not even from spiritual teachings – but from lived experiences that came to show me the way in the years to come.

# CHAPTER 5

## Shooting for the Moon

*"If you want the moon, do not hide from the night."* (Rumi)

During those early working years, I met friends, shared stories, learned about people, but most importantly, I discovered something about myself that was to mould my life. In fact, it broke the mould from which I believed all people had been cast. That is not to say I suddenly felt 'special', it was just that I found myself to be a 'degree south of different' in one significant respect. Yes, I had already seen some differences by this stage – I had noticed that other people weren't apparently seeing and feeling anything other than what was in front of them. That had been strange to me, but it hadn't had a name. It was now that it fully dawned on me that people were not Mediums who obeyed their own traffic lights, they just weren't Mediums at all.

This realisation came in a very normal, though surprising, place. I was sitting with friends in a pub having a Babycham (Mother would not have approved). There I was, 16 years old, sitting opposite a young man called Tim. I hadn't seen him before in our small community, and I would have remembered, because he just happened to be a modern-day, young Brad Pitt. I was smitten and desperate. I was completely out of my depth, I knew I had nothing – clothes that had my home-spun style written all over them, with well-used flat shoes and, to top it off, I was carrying a good layer of puppy fat.

On top of those unfashionable, physical attributes, and being faced with this blue-eyed boy, I was now acutely aware of my own lack of personality too. I just didn't know anything. I couldn't talk about music, art, drugs, sex, anything interesting. I had nothing, but my imagination. So, there I sat, and my mind was working on a story. I knew if I could just gain his attention, there could be a connection and he might 'see me'… Before I could check myself, I was 'shooting for the moon' – leaning forward to confidently issue a challenge:

"Hey Tim! I bet you, I can tell you exactly what your house looks like!"

Now that was more like it, although it was momentarily buried in light-hearted banter:

"You don't know where he lives, stupid!" …
"Go on with you!" …
"Uh-oh! She's off to la-la land again."

I paused at this last comment as it was telling me, probably for the first time – or at least in a way I recognised for the first time – that friends had in fact thought me a bit strange. Despite this, there was still curiosity on his part and it was all directed at me… I had suddenly become important; faces told me so. Mischievously, or so I thought, I began speaking, all the time thinking, *'I will start my story and they will soon laugh, and he will think I'm funny… people like funny … I was good at playing the fool, wasn't I.'*

However, as soon as I began – visualising opening doors to his house in my head – I actually knew, or thought I knew, what was there. I was in the glass-bottom boat again; I was clear-sighted and knowing where I was going. I peered inside each door and just said what I saw.

"Nice house, Tim," I started. "There are three peaked rooves in the front." I made the shape of a pyramid with my hands as he looked unsure. "White walls, but with black wood." His surprise now registered across that easy face of his. "It looks like a bungalow at the front, but it isn't you know." I noticed an eyebrow shoot upward at this. This house wasn't anything like mine, I mused, or my friends' around the table. This was confirmed when I then saw, in my mind's eye, that he had a proper big hall with doors leading off to other rooms, not the 'straight off the pavement into the front room' layout we all had.

Excited to explore further, I then opened the first door off the hall to see a stripy carpet, dark red wall, big TV cabinet, light wood doors, two of them almost side by side, but with a picture of a mountain on the wall in between; big window. *'This was fun!'*

As my descriptions flowed, so did the young man's nods. No laughing yet. He was either a brilliant actor, or I was spot on.

My attention turned to his kitchen next – it was wide and the tiles on the floor shone, they weren't dull red like ours – dressers and cupboards galore, brasses, pictures, plates. One of the brasses had a horse's head on it and – *whoosh!* – I was outside the back of the house. I saw stables. The idea that 'my special friend' liked horses registered, just as I started to describe them to Tim. There was a black coloured horse and a brown and white patchy one. A single nod to this piece of information. I then heard 'paint' in my head and, before I knew it, I'd translated this in a way that made sense to me – "it looks like it's painted," I said.

"It's a Paint," he corrected, head on one side.

"That's what I said." I assured him, undaunted, although we both knew at this point that I knew nothing about horses.

Two eyebrow acrobatics later, and I finally stopped to register the silence. My friends were watching Tim, as was I. I sat back, half expecting him to wink at me, partner to the conspiracy, and then they would all laugh at this, our game.

However, there remained only a breathless anticipation; inquisitiveness, tinged with uncertainty and, as I continued to look at him, I saw yellow paint peeling off the pub wall behind his head. It seemed keen to meet his aura, as if they had something in common. I grew confused; I didn't know what this meant. This had to end. I was out of my depth. I registered the traffic light in my head.

In that moment, I guessed my friends round the table were trying to work out whether I'd been as accurate as Tim's face suggested, or maybe how we knew each other and, perhaps, when we had decided to play this game and play them all for fools. I was working through the options in my head when pandemonium broke out:

"Wow!" he exclaimed finally. "How did you do that?"

I laughed. I heard:

"Can you do that to me?"
"Have a go on me!"
"She knows your house, Dummy! Do me!"

For the boy's part, he still hadn't smiled, nor had he asked me if I knew his family. I realised he had said very little throughout until just. That thought made me laugh again. I don't know why.

The question of 'why I was laughing', as well as the question of 'how I was doing that', were not resolved, as the pub doors suddenly flew open and a post-football crowd loudly invaded the bar. There was jostling and barging, as they were funnelled through the doorway. The uproar chased away the thoughts still hanging in the air and the smell of chips that followed them in filled the senses.

Suddenly, the appetite for food was stronger than the appetite for answers and my young friends were ready to leap from one high energy experience to another. It's the way of teenagers – as if they'll find the holy grail of adulthood somewhere in that leap.

So, 'our bit of fun' was over for my friends at least. For me though, I felt as if I'd opened something in me, opened it wide, and it wouldn't go back in its safe place. It was the first time I'd played my 'mind game' in the big wide world and I'd felt the fear of exposure, so I'd laughed, of course I'd laughed; probably a bit too long, as I retreated inside to have a look at me:

*'This game I played with Mother worked with him too … But there was more - they couldn't do this thing, could they? Not at all. Could no-one else do this, except perhaps that Medium I'd seen?'*

I became conscious of their chatter again. They had decided to share chips and a Vimto and argue about what film to see the following Saturday, while I was to take my leave – loudly, joyously, without a seeming care in the world – and hurry home for my 8 o'clock curfew. They all knew what Mother was like, so they never questioned my decision.

When I got home, and omitting the fact that I had been to a pub, I told Mother all about it. I told her I was a little frightened, I let it all flow out. I wanted to understand what had just happened; I wanted to know what a paint horse was; I wanted to understand my place in the world; I wanted it to be a safe place. Above all else, I wanted her to help me.

She did. In the only way she knew how – at arm's length.

# CHAPTER 6

**Safe Harbour**

*"The most beautiful thing we can experience is the mysterious; it is the source of all true art and science."* (Einstein)

The source of this help was found not too far away in Selly Oak, where a Spiritualist meeting took place in the basement of a high street shop. I was going to a place where it was safe to be me and it was there I met a little, wiry man, who was all of 4 feet 11 inches tall.

He stood in the centre of the people gathered – 15 old women sitting in a circle. He muttered some unintelligible words and I remember wondering if they were foreign, and then he launched into an extensive description of the personal lives of several of the women there. They all seemed happy with the attention, with the 'messages'. No fear here. There was chatting, nodding, clucks of appreciation and awe, no *'cross my heart and hope to die'* … and no laughing either.

We sang hymns, said prayers, just like before, and just like a conventional church service, except for this 'communication with spirit' thing, called 'messages' and they came from 'a higher plane'. It was all very mysterious. These messages came through an intermediary, called a 'Guide' and seemed to belong to the Medium, a sort of mediator between those people on the 'spiritual plane' and the people in the room.

The terminology and setting in the early days was very King Arthur's Round Table set in The Dursley's cupboard under the stairs; a sense that great things were taking place in very humble surroundings. This lofty magic was profound enough for me to want to be part of this secret society and to wonder, for the very first time, if my 'special friend' were *my* Guide?

There was also no sign of the sickness that had plagued me on my first visit and so there was nothing to stop these visits becoming a routine thing for Mother and me. In fact, I looked forward to them more and more. I found kindred spirits, people who didn't think me strange. I never heard anything that worried me, it felt natural. There were no dark corners, candle-lit spectres or croaky voices; nothing spooky at all in fact.

Most importantly for my development, the small, wiry Chairman always allowed others to 'have a go' after the service.

"Did you get anything?" he would ask us in turn.

I very quickly grew in confidence and, invariably, said I had something to say. He would acknowledge with a perfunctory nod and then I would pick someone and tell them things about their lives, or I would even feel prompted to predict something in their futures.

Over several weeks, these predictions seemed to come true, the women would tell my mother (often as if I wasn't standing there) things such as, 'she was right, the house came back on the market, even though we'd given up on it.' Or, 'it was amazing, she knew my sister had passed in August.' Or, 'I still can't believe it, the house number she said, it's where I was born and I didn't know until an Aunt told me, so she couldn't have read my mind could she?'

I became quite a feature, truth be told. Can't say I didn't like it, it was growing on me. More importantly, those whispering successes brought me to the attention of a very important woman; a woman to whom I owe much.

"And this," said the Chairman one evening, looking particularly pleased with himself, "is Mrs. Dorothy Charge, Phyllis."

I eyed the woman. She was softly rounded, but seemed a bit stern and stiff for all that. I decided she was like an old white statue with big alabaster hands. Yet her hair was white, wispy and soft and I imagined she'd be like that inside.

"And this," said the Chairman encircling me with a sweep of his arm, "is our Phyllis. Phyllis has potential!"

This ancient monument looked at me and, in her way, which was both quiet and commanding, she said to my mother:

"On Thursday night, you will bring her to my house in Bourneville and we will sit and talk and we shall see."

And that was that. I was duly passed into the safe harbour that was 'Mrs. Charge' (as I always called her) who proved to be charge by name and in-charge by nature. By reputation, Mrs. Charge was an established Medium in her late 60s, early 70s (I wasn't going to ask which). She had a dear friend who lived nearby, called Phoebe.

Phoebe was a healer; a gentle, soft personality, who organised Mrs. Charge's busy schedule. So Phoebe would usher me in on our Thursday nights, make tea, love me, and Mrs. Charge would teach me. That was to be the way of things for over four years. I came to love them both very much.

Surprisingly, for such a strong woman, Mrs. Charge never forced her views on me. In fact, she said, or did, very little, apart from a prayer to begin our sessions. Much, much later, she confided in me that her Guide had told her that I was 'a delicate flower' and one who should be 'handled with care'.

And handle with care she did.

I was given no other guidelines, other than to relax. She never told me to sit up straight, put my feet flat on the floor, or any other such instructions proffered to many aspiring Mediums of the day. As for 'opening the Chakras', never heard the words, let alone understood what they meant.

What Mrs. Charge gave to me, was the greatest gift one human being can give to another – she gave of her time and her care; free of charge and free of advice, dogma or constraint. For someone like the young Phyllis Hughes, with all her insecurities about her abilities, she could not have handled me better. Thus, swathed in this aura of peace, of security and shielded by this strong woman's wings, I was allowed to flex my own wings, flying off into another consciousness.

The only questions Mrs. Charge would ever ask were variations on the same theme:

"What are you thinking about now?"

Obviously, both Mrs. Charge and friend, Phoebe, were used as subject matter for messages, and much of my awareness was centred on the colours surrounding them and how they were feeling. Sometimes, during my meditations – she didn't call them that, she would refer to 'going into the quiet' – I would become so disassociated with the present and with my physical surroundings, that I would have real trouble returning to my consciousness. This is because I found it so easy to meditate in her presence. It was an effortless transcendence.

At these times, this great, silent, bespeckled woman would place her large hand on my brow and back I would come (it felt like immediately) to find her gentle touch. She had such energy in that touch and I was always aware of her power – her 'charge' – aware of her just being in the room and I always felt safe.

During my time with Mrs. Charge, I began to feel more comfortable with my 'abilities', with the fact that I was, indeed, different. I started to accept this as part of me, although I was never happy with the idea of it as a 'gift', as some were, because it brought with it some acute awareness that I could have lived more than happily without it.

I still feel this way, but when something is effortless, it's difficult to make a decision not to do it. The 'it' is, of course, usually referred to as 'clairvoyance', and I believed that everything I was 'seeing', or becoming conscious of in these sessions, was absolutely correct. No doubts. I didn't know how lucky I was in this certainty. For those around me, I was a 'Natural Medium', but, in hindsight, I now know I was a bit arrogant too; the ego was alive and kicking.

The definition of a Natural Medium – so far as I am aware – is one who can easily use their intuitive sense. However, where the information comes from, that enters that part of the mind deemed intuitive, is a very moot point. Such views tend to vary from 'reading body language', to 'telepathy amongst the living', to 'evidence of a spirit world' and 'life after death'. I can only give you my own view, based on my lived experience, but for now, I would just say that intuition, as such, has a breaking point – it isn't a sound description of what's going on. Such contemplation led me to slowly, but surely, begin to form a vague outline of my beliefs in a consciousness beyond my own and I wanted to investigate it fully.

To do this, it seemed to me that I had to disassociate myself from everything and everyone, so I could stop listening to the outside world and have my own enlightenment. It was something I felt very strongly about. It felt like I needed to 'go away' in every sense. This was to be a full-blown shift and a full-blown dive into the deep and, 'Phyllis being Phyllis', I was incapable of doing anything by halves. No, this was to be an epic journey into self and it required a grand gesture …

…It took me seven months to collect the necessary papers to work in America. I had decided to go to New York!

As excited as I was to get going with this adventure, I was not so keen to leave the loving, safe care of Mrs. Charge. So, when the time came, I hesitated, but I knew all the while that she would not interfere, she never had. All she'd ever done was to teach me about offering others the gift of understanding, the gift of freedom to be; it was her total belief in free will that she imparted to me.

The only person she would defer to was her Guide and so she would say:

"Speak with *your* Guide, Phyllis."

Never, 'you're wrong' or 'don't be silly' or even, 'a little less arrogance perhaps…'

She guided me in this way until I was 21 and until I decided to leave for America. And throughout our time together – and even when her protégé finally took a church service on her own – she never took an ounce of glory for her selfless teaching.

I never saw her again. She faded out of my life as inconspicuously as a door quietly closing, but before she did, on our last day, she said something strange, something I would come to understand in time – in Times Square in fact.

"Go out and be tested."

And I was. New York was to be a place of growth, transformation, reconciliation and a test of what I truly believed. It all but brought me to my knees. What Mrs. Charge seemed to know was something of what was in store for me there, but not even she could have understood what my Guide knew was coming and why. No-one was to know this until much later. For now, and on the face of it, the trip culminated in Times Square with three cents in my pocket, waiting for a woman I'd met just once; needing her to turn up more than I needed breath, but would she come?

# CHAPTER 7

## The Trade Winds

*"Twenty years from now you will be more disappointed by
the things that you didn't do than by the ones you did do.
So, throw off the bowlines, sail away from safe harbour,
catch the trade winds in your sails. Explore, Dream,
Discover."* (Mark Twain)

One bright July morning, exactly three days after my
twenty-first birthday, I flew away like the fledging I truly
was. I remember the world famous Expo '67 was due to be
held in Canada the following year and I wondered if I'd be
home by then. After that thought, my head was in the
clouds even before the Boeing 707.

I sat in a window seat and watched those clouds making pictures for me. It was exhilarating, mind expanding and, of course, solitary and, unbeknown to me, it was to be pivotal to my spiritual development.  For now though, I was happy in this new world, quite sure footed, off to lands anew, pastures fresh. What could go wrong?

Fortunately, I came back down to earth (not so very long after the plane) when I found that the terms and conditions assured by the Agency (who had secured my position as nanny to my American employer) were less than accurate. It had started off well enough. I was picked up at the airport by the family's chauffeur, which was thrilling, although it quickly became clear that he wasn't the sort you spoke to, so I exchanged a few pleasantries and then sat quietly in the back. Truth be told, I was also feeling a little overawed by the white Mustang and its red leather interior, having been driven to the airport in Father's Ford Allegro.

However, seeing the Mustang for the first time was nothing compared to catching sight of our destination – an absolutely magnificent mansion situated somewhere between Woolworth's and the Kennedy's homes on Long Island. This was the only piece of information offered by the chauffeur when, as if by magic, the gates swung open and he smiled for the first time, as if pleased by his apparent sorcery. As I gazed, I compared it to my home in Birmingham and, with some irony, I felt sure they would have a rather larger sitting room and their children wouldn't be sharing bedrooms.

Indeed they were not. After a quick tour, I was shown to my room by a woman who announced that she was Mrs. Bloom's secretary and that Mrs. Bloom would be by later in the day to outline my duties. It was a pleasant, sunny room overlooking the expanse of drive; a drive that disappeared out of sight and you just knew you'd be out of breath by the time the gates showed up.

I had unpacked and displayed, and re-displayed, my few toiletries in the bathroom and I was just wondering if it would be rude to have a look round on my own, when Mrs. Bloom arrived. My first impression stuck of this blonde, perfumed and meticulously fashioned woman – she had the sort of mannerisms and demeanour that said, *'I'm intolerably busy, every day, no exceptions, I don't know how I do it, don't bug me,'* except she really wasn't. There were a lot of sweeping gestures and flappy hands, but very little substance in that expressive aura of hers.

Obviously, the writing was on the wall – as Mrs. Bloom was so very busy, I had to pick up the slack – a lot of it. I very quickly found out that, apart from being nanny to their three children, the Blooms expected me to cook and clean for the whole family. Fortunately, they did have a gardener, otherwise I seriously think I would have been required to don boots and get to grips with the extensive grounds.

After six weeks with this family (and nine bathrooms later), I'd reached new heights of worthlessness. As well as exploring my resilience, I explored every nook and cranny of their residence – had Ajax been a face cream, I would have emerged from the experience with at least a new identity.

Fortunately, at this point, the old Phyllis surfaced magnificently in the face of such adversity; anger finally overpowered the echoey silence that had fallen all about me since my arrival, so that the awe-inspired insecurities fell away and off I marched to the nearest phone booth and called the Agency:

"If you don't do something NOW, I'll write to my MP and anyone else I can think of! I'll tell them you've got me out here under false pretences! It's slave labour!" I proclaimed finally.

Not a very inventive speech, but my passion made up for it and it seemed to work, as the Agency offered an alternative position of nanny to another family living on Long Island. Synchronicity popped in at this point (like a good neighbour) as the contact's first name turned out to be 'Grace'. The familiarity of Mother's name made me feel hopeful.

"Hello, is that Grace Dubrovsky?" I asked.

"Why yes," I heard.

"Good! I'm Phyllis Hughes, the Agency gave me your number, you need a nanny," I told her with breathless anticipation.

We exchanged a few pleasantries at this point. This was no mean feat given my desperation – and risky too, as we were both trying to read each other's characters at that moment. (I could feel this intensely and it was debilitating). Despite the tension, we arranged to meet briefly the next day.

Oh my! It was a long night. There was hope on the horizon now, but panic in the foreground. I tossed and turned, moving between waves of elevated emotion and pit-black despair. I kept thinking, *'there's nothing to go home for, I can't go back a failure, but there's nothing to stay for either…'*

By the next day, I was in a terrible state and this was to be my excuse for my next action. I walked up to this woman called Grace, in our pre-arranged meeting place in Times Square, and the first words out of my mouth were:

"Are you Jewish?"

I really don't know why Grace didn't walk away from me right then, but she didn't. I think she could see a frightened child in a young woman's body. I think she saw the loneliness in the plump face, the vulnerable green eyes and the panic in the blank stare. For whatever reason, she gave me time to explain why I'd asked and I did. In a rush, I told her all about Raguel and, in return, this wise woman told me all I needed to know about her in the moment of her response.

She told me that people were all different and she would welcome the opportunity to show the other side of Jewish life. She even suggested I came for a brief visit to her house to meet everyone before deciding. However, by then, I'd learned everything I needed to know about the woman called Grace:

"No! I'm quite happy, I'll work for you!" I exclaimed.

So, the next day, after just six weeks of trying to fly instead of getting back in my glass-bottomed boat and trusting the tide, I dragged my small case out of a cab and was left standing, once more, in Times Square – no money, no food, no job, no accommodation and, all of a sudden, no hope. On the basis of one meeting, during much of which I must have seemed deranged – hardly the sort of person anyone would choose as a nanny – I was waiting for the woman, Grace, to just roll up and whisk me and my one small suitcase out of this hellish predicament.

I stood, feeling more alone than I'd done in a long time; imagining what Mrs. Charge was doing, finding some comfort in the domestic scene that filled my mind at that point. I stayed here in my head for a while, then dared myself to go back to searching the crowds for the woman I'd met just yesterday.

I saw her then.

My panic immediately receded somewhat and I took in Grace's appearance, as if for the first time – a solid, yet attractive, well-dressed, dark-haired woman with a jaunty, purposeful walk. She was much taller than me, about 5'6''. I decided she had the look of a Russian gymnast about her – why Russian I didn't know, but that was Grace all right.

When I'd finished flailing around in an inhospitable sea of panic, I found that the Dubrovskys lived in a long dormer bungalow, with a sweeping semi-circular drive on Long Island in an area called Huntington. Not as grand as the Bloom's, but that was of no concern to me. I found that Grace was wife to Greg and mother to Helene and Hannah and she needed a nanny because she was just finishing a training course and then she'd be off to teach full time. The children needed consistent care, that was all – no cleaning, cooking, washing – and I even had the run of the self-contained second floor of their home. (It had originally been converted for Grace's mother, but she had decided not to lose her independence in the end).

As I explored my own, beautifully furnished, living space, I kept asking myself, *'is this real?'*

I think this was to be my downfall – lack of faith. My belief was just too shallow to allow me to float gently with the current, I kept bumping into rocks, kept getting grounded; I'd hop off the boat and put my feet on solid ground thinking I was safe, only to find myself out of my depth the next moment. I hung on like this, leeward, for three weeks before losing my footing again as, out of the deep blue, Grace confided in me that she had decided she didn't want to teach after all.

We were in the family kitchen and, as often happened, Grace was making tea in the samovar, a sort of ornately-decorated Russian tea urn. One of the first things we'd done together when I'd arrived was to drink tea and it had started us talking about Grace's family. Her grandparents had fled Russia to Germany and then, before the war, they'd escaped to America. This samovar had come with them and been passed down. She explained that it wasn't only a focal point for Russian family gatherings, but her grandparents had believed, as many Russians had, that samovars had souls and could communicate with people.

Although Grace cared deeply for others and was very spiritual, I don't think she believed this, but she did hold it dear as a precious artefact of her ancestors and, like those before them, the Dubrovskys were heavily into tea-drinking. I don't remember it ever being cold.

I turned cold though as Grace replaced her cup and admitted that she really wasn't sure what she was going to do. My head clouded with panic, a now familiar sensation, as I realised that my services would no longer be needed.

After such a lot of bliss in such a short time, I was to find myself potentially unemployed and homeless again. I was holding my breath a lot over the next twelve hours as Grace pondered. I know this because I was playing hopscotch with the children and nearly fainted.

This decision must have been hard for Grace too, as by now, I had come to know her to be a thoroughly dependable person; one who thought deeply about others and I had also, finally, come to recognise that this was largely to do with her Jewish heritage.

As luck would have it, I was to find out that Grace had come to value our friendship by this stage and husband, Greg, loved me like a sister, while I had become a most beloved aunt to the children. So, again over tea, this dependable, kind woman announced that the family had unanimously decided to keep me on. The arrangement was, I would pay for my board and lodging just by baby-sitting a few nights a week.

Ok, so now I could breathe and believe my luck too. I was in full sail again, everything going my way. Importantly, this was the very freedom I needed to spend time in self-contemplation and introspection, although it started with me watching TV for two days and two nights solid. In my defence, it is worth remembering we only had the BBC at home at that time, so 15 channels (if I remember correctly) was some sort of miracle. After this vigil, I decided I really didn't like watching TV after all, so I turned my gaze elsewhere. Upwards, in fact.

Now, I had time and space to experiment and build on my relationship with my spirit friend. I called him into my everyday life by asking questions, I tested, I played games:

"What's going to happen today?" I would ask aloud.
Then I'd listen, wait for 'it' to happen. This ethereal communication (somewhat indefinable, in-your-head type

of talk-talk) occupied me, as it always had done, but now I was more focussed and determined to refine my skills, so I would ask for a more precise timescale, or more detail.

It really wasn't hard for me to communicate like this, although I later learned (when sitting in mediumship development circles with others) that people really struggle with this. They struggle with knowing who's talking in their heads – doubting, challenging, drowning in streams of consciousness. Of course I didn't appreciate that then, it was just…well, I knew *my* head-talk and I knew *his*.

It was just about this time, when I'd exhausted the potential of these tests – I mean, just how many different sort of things can happen on your own, in one place – when Grace presented me with a charcoal sketch pad and some paints for my birthday. I don't know why – possibly my love of colour and stories of the Rosenbergs? I certainly suspect she thought I needed occupying.

That gift opened up new avenues of expression for my experiments. I thought, *'if my Guide could give me details of forthcoming situations, conversations and events, could he make these details come to life in a drawing and communicate that way?'* I'd got this idea from hearing someone talk about 'automatic writing' at the Selly Oak Spiritualist meeting one night and, although unsure of the details, I was pretty sure this was the same sort of thing.

So it began. I would sit in my living room and begin to doodle. It wasn't very productive at the start, so I then began copying pictures in an effort to get things moving and to get used to using paint. One in particular comes to mind as I relate this – a Chinese-style picture of a nightingale sitting on a branch. When I sat back to look at it, it was remarkable, I was truly amazed. For someone who had shown no previous artistic talent in this respect, it was frankly unbelievable.

One night, when all was quiet in the house, I was inspired to just let go of the helm; let go of trying to copy things and allow my mind to be still. I didn't even think of anything to paint, I just let my hand move freely in the way that I thought automatic writing would work.

Very quickly, or so it seemed to me, there appeared one glorious portrait of an indigenous American Indian. I set it down to look at it. I walked about eyeing it from every angle – magnificent head dress, detailed in individual feather and minute bone and executed with a skill I knew nothing about. The eyes particularly drew me in and I 'knew', inexplicably, undeniably, that this was my Guide.

Although enthralled, it struck me as odd that he was a North American Indian. I wondered if this were why Mrs. Charge never mentioned this to me – did she think it odd too? Did she think it would alarm me? I really wasn't worried, possibly because I'd been 'brought up' on images of Cowboys and Indians on TV – The Lone Ranger, Ponderosa, Gunsmoke, Rawhide – and these stories were full of the imposing half-savagery, half-majesty of the Indian.

That idea made me wonder if Guides appeared to people in ways that made sense of their time and space. I can't say I would have chosen an Indian, particularly as, later, people were to ask me – 'why can't Guides just be ordinary people?'

My Guide was clear about the answer to this – there are those of our world who are far more likely to be Guides; to do this work. They are those who have lived closest to nature, learned to communicate in a broader sense; to commune with the energies of our world and the spirits of the senses. No, I do not find it surprising that my Guide is who he is.

That day though, I was surprised about the name he was to be given. When Grace saw the picture for the first time – and without knowing what he meant to me – she commented on the unusual colour I'd chosen for the feathers. She told me that there were still two reservations on Long Island; that Native Americans had inhabited this island for thousands of years and, in their culture, a blue feather was a symbol of protection and guardianship.

As I listened intently to Grace on how the Indians had migrated west from Long Island, it suddenly dawned on me that wanting to go to America, and ending up here, hadn't been coincidental at all. It had been my Guide's ancestral home and, from that day on, I was to call my Guide what I thought would be an appropriate Indian name – 'Blue Feather'.

The rest of the Dubrovsky family were equally enchanted with my painting, but for different reasons. Unlike Grace, and true to nature, Helene's awe quickly turned to pragmatism – she needed to make a contribution to the school exhibition of art that was being held at the end of that semester and, given the Indian presence on Long Island, she thought it would be an excellent fit. After initial protests from me of 'it's not good enough' were quashed by Grace, I agreed. How could I not listen to Grace? She was 'arty', sophisticated, a woman of the world and if she said it was good then I was completely assured. So, it had its moment out in the world, before it was to take its place on the family's sideboard and I went on drawing, painting and experimenting.

Other than this activity and playing with the children, I didn't do anything really; seems a wasted opportunity now. I rarely ventured out to see the sights. I suppose I could have been anywhere really, but this isolation on my 'long island' was self-inflicted because I was a plump, young woman who didn't fit in with the fashionable culture around her. Too many skinny women and men with little bodies and big heads featured heavily on the TV and in the many glossy magazines dotted around the Dubrovsky home; they even populated the sidewalk outside the house. They were everywhere, so I just stayed put.

At some point, I recognised two things, not only was I fat, but I was also very homesick for familiar surroundings. Despite the kindness of the Dubrovskys, I felt isolated and alone. I couldn't do much about the latter, so I put all my effort into dieting. Made sense to me for reasons I couldn't quite put into words and I committed fully. Exactly when determination turned into obsessiveness is a difficult thing to pinpoint, but after a few weeks, I noticed I was lethargic, achy and bruising very easily.

I told Grace about my symptoms of course – good, reliable Grace who had saved me twice – and to my surprise, she immediately sprung into action. I think she had been on the edge of intervening, as she had noticed my lethargy and the fact that my hearty appetite had declined. She contacted a friend of her mother's and they had secured an appointment for me to see a specialist in New York within days … her mother had friends everywhere!

So one of the few times I ventured into the big city, I was left breathless, not with amazement, or excitement, but with shock. I found out I had … Leukaemia.

*'See?'* I muttered under my breath, still in a daze, as Grace drove us home in silence, *'that's why I don't go anywhere'. 'No good comes of it'. 'What had I done to deserve this?'* I mused. *'Maybe I hadn't worked hard enough with Blue Feather? Was it punishment?'*

I felt Grace's side glance and I stopped muttering to stare solemnly out of the car window. In reality, I was devastated, I felt deserted, dissolute, betrayed. I was going to die …

Still too shocked to cry, I prayed quietly then. I realised that it was these times, when all the knowledge of life beyond material existence, just didn't hack it. Well, not when you're in your 20s. One thing I was to learn that day – if you lose your faith, you lose grace, certainty, peace, salvation – it's a fathomless abyss into which we sink at our peril.

"Wait for the test results," Grace said out of the blue, knowingly, reassuringly. "We don't know for sure, he just said we should be prepared…"

We went back to silence. I went back to prayer.

That night, the Dubrovskys gathered round, distracting me with Monopoly and pizza and Coca Cola and then Medovik and Pechenye Yabloki (honey cake and baked apples). The pizza was especially for me and the puddings were, I suspect, the most calorific and quick to prepare Grace could think of while keeping an eye on me.

The Dubrovsky's commitment to family life was my idea of a worldly heaven. One, I realised, I longed for.

The next day, the phone rang mid-afternoon. It was for me. As my diary wasn't bursting with friends and acquaintances, I knew it must be the doctor. Anyway, I knew his voice immediately. I confirmed this to Grace with a nod. Grace leaned in to listen. I imagined him sitting at his desk, surveying the results, working out how to tell me. I could hear his lips part again to speak.

"They're clear."

I hear the tough-sounding Brooklyn accent, but not the words at first. I'm in a half space between dreaming and living and then I start wondering if my blood's *'clear'* due to a total absence of any red blood cells?

Grace senses my half-life:

"The results are clear, Phyll."

Grace took the phone from me then and let it register. It did, but it's odd what we think at the worst of times – *skinny and alive!* I was at the peak of a glorious, warm wave that was rushing through my senses and telling me that I had never been so alive as now. As a result, I didn't hear much of Grace's conversation until, that is, I became aware that her head was nodding enthusiastically. I remember thinking that her enthusiasm was telling me she was trying to 'wrap things up' with him and get off the phone. Finally, I heard:

"Thank you James, we're delighted." This was followed by a "yes of course, I will" and "Mother's appointment is in three weeks, yes?" Then she replaced the receiver quickly and hugged me. It was a long one.

"No more fad diets for you Phyll," she cautioned, as she released me from her bear hug and led me into the kitchen. She fired up the samovar and related what the doctor had said.

Apparently, I had Vitamin K deficiency, a symptom of which is bruising easily – also a common symptom of Leukaemia, but its other common symptoms of lethargy and aching were just the result of starving myself.

*Couldn't you just die…*

# CHAPTER 8

## The Priest

*"You have to grow from the inside out. None can teach you, none can make you spiritual. There is no other teacher but your own soul."* (Swami Vivekananda)

Next day, I went to the beach!

Admittedly, this wasn't purely a reaction to feeling intensely alive – and fortunate, and grateful, and seeing everything so vividly that I couldn't get enough – more like Grace was nagging me to get fresh air. Oh and I was now thin enough to make a public appearance!

There I lay, propped up on one elbow, listening to the surf rushing up to the shore, whispering something just to me, then chuckling to itself, as it scattered the sand this way and that. I was so happy. It was peaceful, so quiet, the beach practically deserted.

Deserted, apart from a young priest making his way along the shore. He was short of stature with straight dark hair, a hand thrust into his cassock pocket and he walked slowly, as if the world had settled on his strong shoulders and could rely on him. It registered as 'odd' to see a priest on the beach that particular day and, although I'm sure he was real, that wasn't what concerned me. I was really thinking how sad it was that he would be denied the laughter and wonder of marriage, children – a family, like the Dubrovskys.

This led me to wonder what Sophie and Patrick were doing. I'd received a letter recently talking about Christmas plans and reading in between the lines – on how Sophie had a boyfriend and how Patrick was as sporty as ever, but now learning accountancy at night school – I could tell Mother wasn't happy about me spending another holiday period in America. You didn't have to be a Medium (natural or otherwise) to pick up on that.

I had been on my long island for 16 months now and the pangs of homesickness had increased. It was time to go. It felt as though there was nothing else to be done.

I sensed a good decision had just been made. I tilted my face up to the sun; shut my eyes, peace and contentment shining through me and clearing all thoughts in its bright light.

Suddenly, I heard:

"Enjoy the rest of this time child, because, when it has passed, you will work throughout this earthly life."

My eyes opened. I scanned the sands for the priest. I couldn't see him and, at that moment, my brain registered the sound of the voice in my head – it was Blue Feather and I knew he wasn't talking about the work of many, he was talking about mediumship. I was just wondering why he had decided to interrupt my priest-filled peace when, very quickly, I was filtering information at a rapid pace.

Although some experiences are destined to be trapped by words, I can only say, if a computer could feel, it would feel something like this when it had a 'download'. It was pure conceptual flow, no spoken words, but a storyboard of knowing, using every cell in my body for energy, or so it seemed. My senses were alive with the pulse of the tide and the blood running through my veins. I knew everything in such a rush, and with such insight, that I suddenly knew *absolutely nothing at all*. I soared up to the stratosphere, saw the landscape of my journey to New York splayed out beneath me and was speechless at what Blue Feather imparted to me.

He told me that it was the custom of his people (the Lakota, Sioux) to send the young out on their own into the wilderness on a 'vision quest'. A time when the young sought guidance from their ancestors; it was a solitary journey into the self and its connection to the spiritual realm when they faced challenges, they fasted, prayed and meditated.

I may not have found seclusion in a sacred mountain or desert, as he had done, but New York's Long Island had been my wilderness, no doubt about it. I had disconnected from worldly distractions and immersed myself in introspection in full sight of a strange, new world. My journey had been custom-made for me – a young woman who didn't possess the skills to cross a wilderness on her own, but who needed solitude nonetheless, because she just wasn't ready to declare her gifts to the world. Yet, as custom-made as it was, my experiences had aligned with his. I had experienced solitude, challenge, fasting and communion with the spiritual forces around me; I had lost self-worth with the first family, felt utter panic and desperation, found grace, meditated, been drawn into contemplation with my Guide, fasted and, finally, faced my own mortality. Little had I known, when I had stepped off the plane that day, that the first people to ever inhabit Long Island were Indians and this sacred ancestral home was to be my wilderness, my vision quest too.

A beautiful truth left my eyes swimming in the most ecstatic joy as enlightenment dawned. Like a deer in the wilderness, there was just sensing; I had learned a little about communing with the energies of our world and the spirits of the senses.

I thanked my teacher, my Guide, my friend, for his presence, felt his strong heart telling me all was well and I knew my struggle was over. I was truly awake and I had learned one of the greatest lessons – I'd learned I was fallible. Fallibility is difficult to teach someone by putting thoughts in their heads, or in their dreams – it's an emotional response gained through lived experience by a physical, emotional mind and stored in the scars of a physical body. That's just the way it must be – you have to grow from the inside out and you have to journey from the head to the heart.

I was to leave my island with the same confident spirit, but there was something more discerning about me, more refined. The brashness had gone and empathy had taken its place. For now, at least, I was back in the boat, in the flow downstream, and a little nearer – spiritually speaking – to becoming a fisher of men.

# CHAPTER 9

## Back on Earth

*"We are not human beings having a spiritual experience.*
*We are spiritual beings having a human experience."*
(Pierre Teilhard de Chardin)

As I step off the plane the next day, I fall to earth as Mother and Father greet me – lofty thoughts gone and I look at Father's new car – an Austin 1100 – and wonder: *'how are we going to fit in that?'* American cars were so much bigger! Fortunately, I didn't have to worry about how Sophie, Patrick and I were to fit into one bedroom again, as they had moved while I'd been in America and so I would only have to share with Sophie.

As Father drove us to our new home and back to see my brother and sister, I chatted away in an effort to fill the quiet that was between my parents – their love had finally fallen through the cracks in their silences.

Despite my reservations about home life and what was to come, the minute we got home and I saw everyone all together, the familiarity was overpowering. It felt safe. No, I would not be returning to America. It had served its purpose. I was awake.

This certainty was all I was to take home from my 'quest' that Christmas, for my one and only trunk, containing all my 'worldly goods' – which I sent by boat because it was cheaper – got diverted to Antwerp. I told myself then, that I had been right to leave the portrait of Blue Feather on a mantelpiece of the Dubrovsky's home, although I knew the truth was, I was not ready to explain him to anyone.

We arrived home and I remember my brother, Patrick, being so emotional that he'd had to go out into the garden to compose himself. That was Patrick's quiet way. Sophie seemed pleased to see me too, although she was clearly preoccupied. I later learned she was serious about her boyfriend and was soon to leave home. I guess part of her had already left that day.

Nonetheless, I enjoyed a wonderful three weeks, encompassing Christmas and everything it brings – more openness, sweetness, hopefulness – I told them all about America and my experiences, although I never told them (or anyone in fact) about my quest, or what transformations had happened within me, or about my painting and my introduction to Blue Feather, so they came away thinking I'd landed on my feet as usual. I'd gained a reputation for doing just that. The alternative was to fill in the blanks and I just didn't want to do that.

Once the Christmas cheer had cleared, along with the Turkey cold cuts, Mother told me in no uncertain terms (no surprises there) that they would not be supporting me any longer. I was hoping for a few more weeks, truth be told, before I had to find a job to pay my way, but *'never mind'* I thought and off I trotted, full of potential, to get a job as a hairdresser.

Don't ask me why, other than it was the next job on my job list. It had occurred to me that a hairdresser would never be short of work and that was a good thing. I had also decided that I was going to be 'quite good at it' for some reason, so, at 22, I was going to have to find an apprenticeship.

Undaunted, I traipsed around the small Midlands town of Droitwich, offering my services to every hairdressers there. Naturally, I was informed I was too old for an apprenticeship (several times in fact). Finally, I came across a 'Mase & Gerards' in the High Street. I'd bypassed this one previously, as it was large, impressive and in a prime position, so unlikely to be short of staff. I sighed and marched in with nothing to lose.

"I don't care what I do! I don't care if you pay me a 16-year old's wages, but I want to learn hairdressing!"

I remembered to smile then. I think the manager, Mr. Thorn, must have been impressed – either with the smile or the audacity – because he told me that, whilst he didn't need another hairdresser, he did need a receptionist. And, if I would do that job and work Mondays (I didn't understand the significance of that at the time), he would teach me hairdressing in his free time. I accepted.

Unfortunately for me, I'd acquired a few Americanisms from my travels that Mr. Thorn didn't appreciate. He didn't like me saying 'yeh ok' or 'sure thing' to customers and, after a week, he told me so. Apart from that objection, I think he liked me and he found I did have a flair for cutting hair. Within a few weeks, as fortune would have it and with perfect timing, one of his hairdressers left and I became a fully-fledged member of the team.

It was during this time that my spiritual hearing developed; my auditory skills, or clairaudience. Previously, I'd seen pictures (clairvoyance), or felt things (clairsentience), and although I would say that I 'heard things', it was rarely audible. It was a thought in my head – it was a conceptual stream of consciousness between two beings and the only way we feel we explain it is by saying we heard something.

However, when I started hairdressing, I actually began to hear – in the usual sense – what was said by those who accompanied the living, so I would chat away to the beings who came with my customers. Of course, my 'chat-back' was inaudible to others around me. Nonetheless, you know you're having a conversation because there's a natural progression to it; a turn-taking, just as if the person were in the room with you.

In time, some of the staff started to ask for advice because they thought I was smart – they'd heard me offer guidance to customers and come to the conclusion I was a bit of a therapist, but really I couldn't have offered them the first sentence on their predicament without my Guide.

We chatted a lot us hairdressers. There seems to be a need to fill silences, but there's also something about hairdressing that opens people up. It is the gentle, quite intimate, therapeutic ministrations involved in hair styling that seems to release inhibition in people. As a result, I was privy to client's great personal triumphs and tragedies.

Fortunately, the hubbub around of other conversations and the sound of machinery – the snip-snip of scissors, the trill of telephones and the hum of driers – meant that my chit-chat-come-counselling continued unchallenged. Every day, or so it seemed, I had opportunities to practise and develop my mediumship in this, the most unlikely of settings.

For that reason, clients, nearby, wouldn't have heard anything startling, they would have heard me start my message with things like, 'have you thought about it this way?' Or, 'maybe you don't have to meet the situation head-on, could you try…'

This is natural mediumship at its best. It's conversational and more therapeutic, but far less recognisable, than the expected afterlife 'sound bites' of: 'I've got Uncle Ted here and he wanted you to have his watch' … 'Your Mum says she misses you' … 'Remember when you cut your own fringe before school?' Nothing wrong with this type of message at the right time and in the right place, but the unsuspecting wider world at this time needed a little more stealth. As a result, I was learning a different way of working in a more modern world, yet one that still wasn't ready to accept mediumship. After all, this was a time before Dr. Raymond Moody had introduced the 'spiritual hereafter' and his concept of 'near-death experiences' to the world. This book was to start to change the way people looked at dying and initiate the debate about the possibility of an afterlife. But, for now, spiritualists were still very much 'in the cupboard under the stairs'.

It followed that, to the outsider, my mediumship had to look perfectly natural – just chatty Phyllis doing chatty work that helped people – but, to me, it was every living proof that I was not alone and nor were they.

Meanwhile, I was living a normal life too – building a social circle, paying my keep, getting on pretty well at home, enjoying being part of a family again, although Sophie moved out during this time – no fanfares or dramas – she just did it her way with maximum privacy. Mother kept in touch with her, but we just drifted; unsurprising really, as we were just totally different people who happened to live in the same house. She married, had a daughter and moved to Australia.

Fortunately, Patrick was more like me – a lively, happy child and adult, although he was clever like Sophie too. He had started working in a grocery store as an errand boy before leaving school. After a year, he was managing it, as the manager was killed in a car accident. He did it so well that he was asked if he would go to night school and learn accountancy. So, by this time, he was their chief accountant. He just had a head for business, Patrick.

Things were fairly idyllic really, until, one Saturday, Mr. Thorn announced that all the hairdressers had to buy their own equipment. This was, effectively, a pay cut for us. I wasn't impressed and told him so. In fact, at some point, I told him to 'get stuffed' – yes, I know I said I was more enlightened, less brash, post-America – but this hot-headedness still occasionally surfaced. It's one of the drawbacks of forgetting you're a spiritual being living an earthly life and not the other way round.

Our relationship deteriorated rapidly after my outburst – which was me fighting authority again – until the situation finally hit rock bottom on another, very busy, Saturday, when I'd been overbooked. I found myself with two customers under the driers, I was just combing out another, and a fourth one was waiting in reception. After a few stressful words, on both our parts, I stuck my nose in the air and informed him:

"I shall require my cards by next Saturday."

I think he was a little sorry later, because I really had turned into a proficient hairdresser but, 'Phyllis being Phyllis', there was to be no turning back – impetuous and unemployed again at 25 years of age. After a little regret my end, I decided there was nothing else for it, but to work for myself – I would travel to people's houses.

My thoughts were fairly pragmatic at first – this way of working would transfer well to pretty much anywhere. So, once I had everything I needed, I would be set for life. Luckily, I had built up a good clientele in three years, so I wasn't too worried, except for the financing bit. Fortunately, this turned out ok too – I had some good friends called Ross and Dan and they offered to support me until I got my first wage. As it was, I didn't need it. In the first week, I earnt £8, £11 the second (this is 1970's money!) and, in six months, I was flying.

It was so easy that, as had happened before in my life, when synchronicities popped in like good neighbours, I realised there was a reason for it. It then dawned on me that this way of working would enable me to deliver messages that were far more personal…

*'Maybe my hot-headedness hadn't been 'just me being me' after all? Was it necessary to make me turn my back on a good job?'*

Whether it was or not, all anyone saw around me was that the reputation for landing on my feet was holding fast, but, in reality, this way of working provided a rich and fulfilling few years when I felt useful, as well as blessed. Being in someone's house, with all their belongings around them, and the possessions of those who had gone before, brought a warmth and a depth to the communication.

It is true to say that not everyone wanted to commune with their spirit friends, but often they did. For this reason, these were some of the most rewarding times of my life and they tell us that Mediums *are* everywhere – look at the message, not the messenger – find the angel in the answer, don't look for the angel first, you'll see a fallible human being and it will stop you in your tracks.

The happiness of this, my working life, was matched by my personal one. I had acquired new friends and was actually going out and enjoying myself more. I'd made extra effort, as Patrick had moved out to marry and they'd gone to live in Burton-on-Trent. I was still missing Patrick when, one Saturday night, I went out as usual only to find myself a husband!

It was a week before Valentine's Day and the minute I looked at this man, I knew I'd marry him. There was something comfortingly familiar about him – fairly short, about my height, straight dark hair, a hand thrust into his trouser pocket and broad shouldered, although, if I'm honest, a bit stooped – I think he was going for the 'casual' look.

As I examined him, I felt all those emotions that make the leap worthwhile but, at the same time, I could see it was going to be a double-edged sword – I wanted this man, but I valued my independence and, like my mother before me, I was still faced with balancing domestic chores, childcare and paid work. And what would he think of my 'real work' – my relationship with Blue Feather?

As I gazed into his green eyes and forgot all my questions, I suddenly remembered my thoughts about marriage and the young priest that day on the beach. It seemed they had turned out to be more prophetic than dreamy.

# CHAPTER 10

### The Priest and the Hairdresser

*"A happy family is but an earlier heaven."*
(Sir John Bowring, commonly ascribed
to George Bernard Shaw)

A man called David Albutt married me on the 3 April 1971, and the wind blew so hard, as we walked out of the Church, that the photographer had to put a stone on my veil to hold it down. Fortunately, the storm didn't bother me, I felt as though I was holding a good course and everything would be ok. All my previous concerns had blown away and, when the sun did shine that day, it felt delightful on my upturned face; as warm as me inside.

These were quiet days when feet were firmly planted in the physical world – when David and I worked very hard to save the money for our first house – David, as a psychiatric nurse, me, as a hairdresser. When we made it, we couldn't afford to eat, let alone go on honeymoon. It didn't matter to me. I was so happy.

We had a blissful 12 months getting to know each other and although I had thoughts about what David would make of my secret life, it was a non-event for us – those early days were just about making a home for us and I loved it. It was my space to govern my way. After that, we got down to the real business of working at being married. We still are.

Even in those early days, we were desperate for a son and, in June 1972, I gave birth to a lovely baby boy. I called him 'Patrick' ('Pat' for short) after my wonderful brother. I still got to see Patrick from time to time, but both of us were busy – he was still as fit and sporty as ever while being a really successful businessman by this stage – and I was so proud of him. He now also had two children, so we had to be content to love each other at a distance and make the most of our occasional get-togethers.

To Patrick and me, children were important. I can't help thinking this was due to our upbringing. I was asking Blue Feather about raising our children on one of our in-between-housework-chats and he said that 'without roots in solid ground, young saplings dance around in the faintest of breezes'… made me think *'our young forests aren't firmly rooted these days.'*

With so much support all around me, it came as some surprise then (quickly turning into shock) that, at this happiest time in my life, I fell into a deep depression. It was to take 10 months before I could look at my baby with joy, due to post-natal depression. A consequence of living almost entirely in the physical world is, entirely, physical responses.

These feelings were beyond me, it was an out-of-body experience to be so inexplicably sad in the happiest of surroundings. David must have been nonplussed, although he said little; too busy perhaps learning the real meaning of his wedding vows, particularly that sticky bit about 'giving a dam' in sickness ... If I'd ever doubted my decision to marry this man, it stopped here, because he quietly supported me emotionally, and got on with the mundane practicalities of running a home at the same time, while I worked things out at my own pace. A priest among men.

When I finally did work things out, I realised I loved our baby more than life itself and so, when David started to talk about another child, I was immediately and peculiarly, worried that I wouldn't be able to love her, or him, as much. Again, a consequence of living in the physical world, where love is limited.

In addition, I had my mother's example swirling around in my brain, where the inequality of affection was so evident that it tainted every experience it touched. Of course, most people do love their children equally or, at least when they don't, they wouldn't give those thoughts oxygen.

I shouldn't have worried, I did love her. We named her 'Helene' and she was born in November 1973. She was called Helene after Grace Dubrovsky's daughter and would always remind me of a more adventurous Phyllis.

Now, I was in my stride and motherhood was effortless. I loved them scampering around me, offering me endless guided tours of my living room, encircling my fingers with theirs, balancing one on a hip and folding washing with the help of the other. My time with them always felt like a gift, a precious one, and I believe I felt this strongly because it was at this time that I lost my beloved brother.

I knew nothing of it; no premonition and just as well I think. He was 37 years of age. It was the same year as Elvis Presley died – the world lost its music – and I lost mine. He had played sports all his life, yet we were told he died with the heart of an 80-year old.

*An old soul who hadn't been able to part with his most precious gift, his heart.*

At his funeral, I stood with my arm around his wife, sharing our grief, and I whispered, 'he's closer to you now than he's ever been'. She squeezed my arm and managed to dry her eyes, and I went home to hug my children.

I knew then that I needed to cherish all the time we had together. I was determined to be the earthly guide they needed, so they would never doubt themselves, or fear, or lose faith in their abilities, or stop seeing the joys around them. A tall order, but it felt like a calling. As it was, I truly believe that the effort I put into those early years gave them both a strong sense of self and an effortless kindness, because they had been loved and so it came naturally to them to love other people.

That care did not mean I was with them all day though because, after 18 months of the privilege of caring for my children, I had to wrestle with the same dilemma that most '70's women faced – balancing the moral dilemma of leaving young children, nursery costs, domestic chores and needing more money. We were penniless. As torn as I was, I knew what I had to do… I would just have to work harder to care for them after work.

At the same time, and as much as I was fiercely confident that I was going to support my babies – you know that Mother Bear type determination – I had lost a lot of confidence. This was mostly due to having ballooned to 15 stones.

Of course, I'd always been plump, until my American kamikaze dieting regime that is, but now I felt gargantuan – a blobesque Renoir in a Twiggy-inspired world. It hadn't bothered me in my yummy-mummy world, but now I was exposed. Partly, for this reason, I didn't want anything highly visible, nor did I want anything full-time, so I discounted a return to hairdressing. It had to be part-time employment, so I would be home for the children. As a result, I found myself cleaning a local psychiatric nursing home. I found a children's nursery where I could drop them off at 8am and then work till 1pm. Sorted.

I was fascinated by the patients in the nursing home. My mind was full of questions – *'why were they like this? What had happened? How did they get here? Was there no-one to care for them at home?'* I was full of pity and, in the beginning, I found myself being dragged into their emotional maelstrom only to find that, in the flash of a smile, or the seconds it took to offer them a cup of tea, or even in just a blink of an eye, they would change focus; leave me behind with an emotional hangover. I sometimes wondered which world they inhabited in these moments – *'where were they?'*

It wasn't all sadness and introspection though and I learned from the staff that it was ok to laugh with them, as long as it wasn't at them. One of the inmates, called Mary, took to me so well that she wouldn't go for her afternoon nap unless I tucked her up before I went home. A member of staff would say, 'can you see to Mary?' and off I'd go, take her arm and she'd gaze at me with a look that saw everything, expected nothing. In reality, some were just in the next room – metaphorically speaking, like Mary – and some were far away, but all of them needed me to communicate with them on a spiritual level, not through material consciousness.

Time passed with this new understanding, while I cleaned, watched, wondered and my original heartfelt desire to rescue them from this place and cure them all was replaced by the quieter, realistic, disturbing prospect that some of them were not going to get better. The treatment they were getting just wasn't touching them where they now lived. So, I loved them every day and then had to let them go. I couldn't let go of the idea that this had redefined my notions of hell though – it's not a place, but a state of mind.

This experience also affected my views on things, such as alcohol. I drink rarely because I can't give up on clear thinking. I would never be hypnotised; never give control to someone else, and I certainly would never put myself in the hands of a psychiatrist. What would they make of me and my Guide? People who hear voices are not considered 'normal', even when it is a meaningful response to traumatic life events, it is still seen as a 'symptom', not an 'experience' in our world and this had made me wonder if some of the patients at the home had been given a diagnosis of schizophrenia just because they were like me? Once named, could clairaudience ever be normalised again? I doubted it.

Indeed, it is because of this experience that, I have never submitted to any scientific investigation – any scrutiny of a mind that professes to work beyond its physical neuro-chemical boundaries wouldn't end well for me. It is a lesson I needed to learn to keep me safe then, but I knew that, one day, people would have the idea of communication with a discarnate mind in perspective and then they'd start investigating it without reaching for a test tube, or a white coat.

They're here as this biography is being written of course – those from the scientific community and to name a diverse few – Wayne Dyer, Christianne Northrup, Genevieve Davis, Angelo Dillulo, Eben Alexander and Bruce Greyson. Although they do not profess to practise mediumship, their doors are wide open to the unseen, the unknowable, and the idea that the brain is not the mother of consciousness, but the child.

Back in my simple world and after several years of juggling two children, paid work and domestic chores, Pat went off to school and, ironically, I breathed a sigh of relief that some of the responsibility would be shouldered by the school system. *You know that system I hated so much…*

I then spent two days doing nothing, apart from ponder over whether my dear son would reject school as I had done. I hoped that he wouldn't, but I felt that my rebellion against school had as much to do with my upbringing and my developing mediumship as anything else and, in which case, Pat should be fine. He was.

It was around this time that I, like my mother before me, asked something of 'the Great Spirit', as Blue Feather would say. I asked that I be allowed the time to finish raising my children; to have my family in relative peace before working for Spirit in earnest. I was not to work in this way until Pat was 14 in fact.

That's not to say, I ever felt completely alone during that time. It was just that I could choose to 'switch on', rather than being 'switched on'. At these times, I would be speaking to friends and things would just come out about past or future events, or hidden worries – I would then have to find a way of telling them what I'd seen.

Sometimes, it would be as simple as a knack of knowing something was wrong with people and then just offering to listen to their concerns or confusions. This way of working was very familiar to me, as I'd learned it in my hairdressing days although, with friends, I was less inhibited and sometimes I would even tell them what was wrong before they told me.

On many occasions, Spirit used me to give healing to someone, without them even knowing. This healing could be of the mind, or the body, but it was always healing of the spirit, because it's that which dictates the health of both your mind and body.

I voluntarily 'switched on' one day when one of my friends, Lynne (who had known me in the days of Mrs. Charge) and her mother, Mabel, said, 'come and have a session with us'; this was code for clairvoyance and it was to become a regular thing. Lynne would organise a night when we could meet up at her mother's house and read the tea leaves. In fact, Lynne organised everything, even down to buying me a joint of beef, because I would never accept payment. I should say, I didn't really read the tea leaves, but Mabel didn't understand clairvoyance and wasn't comfortable with it, but she was quite happy with the tea leaves idea.

Eventually, Mabel and I drifted apart for this very reason – I stopped pretending that what I was doing didn't involve working with Spirit. I had started to feel uneasy about this distinction, even though Blue Feather never said anything about this particular tea leaves technique; he just encouraged me to work because it gave me opportunities to put my skills into practise. Nonetheless, it did seem to me to trivialise what was actually happening.

I was also remembering my Ouija board lesson, when I'd learned that it wasn't for me. It didn't seem so very different to reading tea leaves now. I wondered whether Mrs. Charge would have approved of either techniques – I suspected not. She had taught me to see worlds through inward contemplation, skilful introspection, not by using external frippery like this. I had forgotten this a few times in my life, even though the message had been clear enough – 'when you place something between pure soul-to-soul transmission, then you defile the beauty of both the message and the messenger – why would you do that?'

Fortunately, Lynne and I stayed friends even after her mother withdrew, and she went on organising 'sessions', except we all knew them as 'clairvoyance evenings' after that and I had, at last, put a 'toe out of the closet'.

Apart from these evenings, and my occasional attempts to meditate on my own and speak to my Guide, I was very much a housewife and mother and happy with my lot. I always have been and truly, left to my own devices, I never would have wanted to be a Medium. It certainly isn't a guarantee of a happy life. In fact, the sensitivity it brings frequently leads to greater hurt through heightened emotional awareness of self and others.

Indeed, I was soon to learn a very important lesson about being a Medium and about being a human being. This lesson is the very same one that aspiring sailors learn when they take the helm for the first time. That is, we survive by the strength of our own moral compass and by our own endeavours. We can't rely on people on earth, or in Spirit, to run our lives for us. We just make choices based on experience and belief and sometimes they're right and sometimes they're wrong.

As a consequence, I firmly believe that we have free will; that there is no fear of retribution from some divine 'overlord', and so we are at liberty to choose to explore our potential for inflicting harm, as well as our propensity to love. It was explained to me as a young woman in this way – consider, if you sit a child at the kitchen table and place a large, sticky chocolate cake in front of them, saying, 'don't eat that'. What is the likelihood of it – or part of it – disappearing if you a) stand over them with a large, swishy stick, or b) leave the room? And which of these two scenarios would give you the greater pleasure as a loving individual? Perhaps more importantly, which of these earthly temptations would your child become the stronger in resisting and, as a consequence, more adept at navigating the world on their own?

The answer seems simple, so why are there people in this world who prefer a watchful, vengeful God – it seems we create God in our own image, not the other way round. In truth, there is no swishy stick, but there is a cosmic law and we know it as 'what you sow, so shall you reap', or 'like attracts like'. It's unbiased, unavoidable, impersonal, and it sometimes takes more than one lifetime into account. The 'Law of Attraction' is, without doubt, the greatest judicial system any civilisation could have imagined. It is not an Old Testament 'eye for an eye' sentiment, but it does invite you to view yourself through the eyes of the other and *feel* what that's like.

I learned this self-determinism because of something that happened next in my timeline – the independent, the formidable, the I-fall-on-my-feet Phyllis was to become wholly dependent on Spirit because of an unexpected visitor. I was to become afraid of making mistakes, of taking the wrong spiritual turn; simply afraid of exercising free will.

Unfortunately, when a child (no matter the age) is learning to sail and just won't let go of your hand to take the tiller, it's not possible for them to move forward, unless you take that hand and place it firmly on the helm. I was to become in danger of never making any decisions myself again and, as I wouldn't let go of Spirit, Spirit had to let go of me. It was a painful time. I can't see it any other way, despite a lesson learned; painful, because I thought my best friend in the world had deserted me.

He hadn't, but Blue Feather had stood back in the shadows, so that the full force of the sun could hit me squarely in the face. So that I would know, it was time to take back control and come home.

# CHAPTER 11

### Pulling the Wings off an Angel

*"Life is made of ever so many partings welded together. Divisions among such must come, and must be met as they come."* (Charles Dickens)

The dream came. A vivid maelstrom of colour, of light; surreal, bright, vibrant. I flowed through the rooms of a house like a will-o-the-wisp, floating, disembodied, but all-seeing. I saw clearly the decoration, the furniture, the way the sun, the colour of ripe corn, reflected off water and shone through expansive windows. The house was not in the UK, I knew that much, but I didn't know where it was, and *why* was I seeing this?

The dream was to come night after night, until I heard the news that Sophie, my sister, was coming home from Australia. Then they just stopped and the penny dropped. We were to meet again.

We'd drifted apart, both of us married, raising children, getting on with our lives. We'd written for a while at first and then I'd grown lazy, lacking discipline. Years passed, oh so quickly and silently, 12 in all.

I, seemingly, celebrated the news by having a minor operation. It appeared unconnected; to have little bearing on this news, but a strange thing happened. I don't know whether it were simply the effects of the anaesthetic, or whether something happened to my etheric body during the operation but, by the time Sophie arrived to stay with Mother in Droitwich, my psyche had gone into hyper-drive. In hindsight, I think that this artificial psychic boost was necessary to equip me for the months to come.

It seemed to me, with my heightened awareness that, even before I could register the news, there she was standing in front of me in my home; bringing a hundred memories back, so that the years apart called to us fondly and we hugged and cried happily. Then, right in the liquid centre of that elation, I had a thought – *'she's come for my approval about something.'* I wondered what, but said nothing.

I then left Mother and Sophie chatting lightly while I made tea. My thoughts chased me down and I was back in our childhood, reflecting on the fact that Sophie had not had an easy one. Perhaps, I had made it worse somehow? Me, with my bouncy, landing-on-my feet vibe, with my jet black hair and ringlet-framed face; a face that fell into a confident, easy grin. My pre-plump childhood days had been kind for me in this respect and I was the one who had received the 'isn't she lovely' remarks from Mother's friends and neighbours. Sophie? *Not so much.*

I stared at my green carpet. I tried to remember what compliments Sophie had received. Had I always been in the sunlight and pushed her into the shadows? Had Mother's treatment of me been so obviously different – I suspected so. In my mind's eye, I could see us in our childhood – she stood, awkwardly, quietly, plainly – a mousey-haired, older sister. As we grew up, Sophie had become a secretary with lace-up shoes, tweeds; an altogether tailored look – aloof, if I'm honest, whereas I had chosen careers that depended little upon qualifications and more on personality. I wore bright colours, ran into the wind; strong willed, arrogant, always wanting to be top dog. If I'm brutally honest, I hadn't had time for Sophie.

*'I was softer now though, more empathic. Perhaps, I could be more to her now?'*

When we finally got to sit down together on our own, greetings done, tea drunk and the metaphorical peace pipe between us, the first thing I found out was that the house in my dreams was, indeed, Sophie's in Australia; true in every detail – of course it was. I knew then, for sure, that something important was about to happen.

Medium or not, I wasn't prepared for what she told me. My sister, who I obviously hadn't known at all, had become a Medium too! She was working in the churches of her hometown. Now, we had something to talk about! Now, the everyday catch-up chit-chat could just fall away and we could sing from the same hymn sheet, maybe even tunefully. Now, we were totally honest with each other, coming to the conclusion that we had both navigated an unruly sea of self-discovery, despite the fact that she was the bright, intellectual one and I, the dumb housewife *(well, not entirely)*.

After this meeting of like minds, it was inevitable that Sophie would move from Mother's and come to stay with me for a while and, during this time, I think she changed her mind a little about me 'just being a housewife'.

This shift really deepened when I took her to my local Weightwatchers meeting one night. I'd joined years ago (after the 15 stone ballooning episode) and had ended up running the programme – quite successfully, even though I say it myself. The bouncy, exuberant show-off in me seemed to attract people and, in fact, the night I took Sophie, there were 100 aspiring slimmers there waiting to be entertained.

Undaunted, I spoke to them, organised and motivated them for an hour-and-a-half and, throughout this, Sophie being a Medium herself, had become aware that I was getting help from Spirit to talk to all these women. I had the strong impression that she couldn't understand why Spirit would bother helping a housewife and a bunch of people to trim their mortal bodies. *'Surely they had loftier matters to attend to?'*

When we talked about it afterwards, I came to realise that she had placed her Guide on one impressive pedestal. In fact, he was so far above her that she could barely reach him. I tried to explain that he would wish to work *with* her; that he was not master and she servant; that her awe-inspiring reverence was making it difficult for him to relate to her on a personal level. I told her that 'worship' was not what he wanted.

*How can you hear the whisper of the trees when you're prostrate on the forest floor?*

Sophie suddenly put up a barrier between us, I could feel it. She didn't want to work this way. She couldn't tolerate the intimacy of such a relationship. She was a 'Christian Spiritualist'; her emphasis was on 'Christian'. She didn't want to imagine for a moment that Spirit wasn't angelic – that Jesus was a spectacular human being, but no son of a discarnate entity who impregnated someone else's wife. This was the stuff of Greek mythology to me, but the sacrament to Sophie and, frankly, it felt like my mother's belief system, not Sophie's.

I had learned that there was humour and earthiness to the kindness of Spirit; that whilst my Guide was undeniably good and kept undesirable energy away from me, his consciousness was not angelic in the formal sense, it was worldly, why wouldn't it be? His feet had walked this earth, but Sophie wanted wings, not feet. I knew we were going to do battle here and now. Not sure why and how we got here so quickly, but we did.

We talked. There was despair, as well as anger. On and on we went into the early hours of the morning. We'd started this about 9 o'clock, after Weightwatchers, and at 5am we were still struggling with our differences. Mine was a pragmatic view of Mediums being conductors of energy – needing to be well earthed to take the charge – with little room for biblical mythology, while Sophie fervently believed in the trinity; every darn story in the book in fact. With me being my pig-headed self and Sophie, with her head in the clouds bathed in glory, where or how could we meet?

Our childhood differences came back to stand firmly between us then; like sentries they guarded the abyss opening up before us. It seemed evident to Sophie that I had been loved by Mother and she had not. Now though, she had the love of Jesus and I, apparently, did not. 'I was arrogant,' she told me (I found it difficult to argue with that) and 'that was my downfall,' she believed. I counter-argued that the love she had from Mother had always gone hand-in-hand with discipline and so her faith must do the same, otherwise it wasn't love as she knew it.

*'Could she acknowledge that?'*

We found no meeting of minds that night and, in fact, it was Blue Feather who called 'time out' in the early morning, when I went out like a light to fall asleep to the dark between us.

Of course that wasn't the end of it by a long shot. It was such an intense time. I felt a huge weight on me to make her whole; so that she could experience uncompromising love, not love held at arm's length by fearful admiration and although I questioned what right I had to challenge her beliefs, I believed everything Blue Feather had ever told me and Sophie's sadness was palpable to me. So, I wouldn't give up, but then neither would she – my very soul was in mortal danger, as she saw it.

We picked up our 'discussions' every evening after that. Such a chaotic time, the strain was immense. I would gather my strength for those evenings, when I learned to lay everything I believed at her feet and let her dismember it, bit by bit, until she found a truth for herself.

In the day, I would be doing household chores, but I wasn't there, I was on autopilot; more aware than I'd ever been that the spirit world was 'just there'. It felt as though I were battling for my sister, but she didn't want me to, she was busy fighting for me.

One night, I pressed one point in particular, which was based on her immutable belief in Jesus as the son of God. I accepted it, watched her relax, but then I asked her to consider that Jesus needed to work through her; to form a compassionate, seamless bond that was summoned with ease, not conjured through reverent incantation, or awe-filled silence.

"Did Jesus ever say 'worship me'?" I asked. "A soul with that depth of love has no ego. Would we change him for our own sakes?" I went on: "for our own sense of misguided propriety?"

*'Could she accept that?'*

The next day, there came the truce at last. It was on our penultimate afternoon together, while we were shopping in Bromsgrove High Street. No more words, just acceptance. How could a small town in the West Midlands know such a cosmic battle was to find peace there? How do any of us know whether the people we pass in the street are having their hopes and dreams break open before our feet? Sometimes they are and this shopping trip was the pinnacle of our time together, breaking to the footfall of the everyday, we walked arm in arm. There could never be a better time for us, never.

I bought Sophie a tapestry of roses to embroider and she took my arm. We had found another interest we shared. With this thought, I can still feel her arm in mine, as we wandered slowly passed the shops. Finally, we were sisters. Finally, we had turned away from the memories and the personalities that remained so very different and we found the spirits of Phyllis and Sophie inside. We were friends already, we always had been.

For three months though, we had gone as deep as you can go into the spirit world, while maintaining a foot in this one. Together, we were joined in spirit to explore and touch each other's very souls. This time brought us closer together than mere mortals could ever hope for in a normal lifetime.

We'd almost pulled each other apart though, but love wouldn't give up on us, it had wings. Actually, I had wondered if it were our Guides who wouldn't give up on us, as sometimes we were just a little too mortal! We were reflecting on this together (now less sisters, more soul mates) when … I saw it! Without warning, a light, like a small white flame, hovered briefly above Sophie and then descended through the top of her head to move deep within her body. I heard Blue Feather speak – there was a baby boy due. He was three months old and that tiny light had represented his spirit joining the physical body in preparation for his earthly life.

Sophie was pregnant! That would come as a shock to say the least, as her daughter was nearly 20 and Sophie, 40. Should I tell her? What would Alan, her husband, say? We walked. I was listening to our footsteps, now in unison. How could I not say this thing? Have this cosmic talk to angel walk along a nondescript high street in a nowhere midlands place; a time and place that, briefly, called us to speak of the everyday from the universal hope. Could I bridge that large void with my small words? Would I spoil everything now?

Still arm in arm, but our sides touched briefly as we fell out of step. I spoke then.

Her glance was not what I expected, there was no hurry, no sudden alarm … was that a half smile? She spoke quietly, saying, rather matter-of-factly:

"You know, I thought I might be, but then I thought it could be the menopause."

Much later that day, this beautiful experience gave me cause to reflect on the spectacular union between the mortal and the immortal being. I cannot say whether we all join our earthly bodies at three months' gestation, it might be at conception for some, but then I rather think that the act of conception is just nature performing its party trick and only the God Force gets to light the candle on that cake.

It also made sense to me that the same spirit light would leave the body at the moment of death, in exactly the same way – so very briefly making angels of us all.

I liked that idea very much. I tried to remember it, so I could tell Sophie the next day which, inevitably, came and she was to leave me. It wasn't to be. Mother and I went to see her off at the airport, but as the moment of departure crept closer and I still hadn't told her, it stuck in my throat – I was choking on it and, at the last minute, I chickened out and hid in the toilets. I just couldn't speak, I couldn't say goodbye. I was having trouble letting her go.

It was like pulling the wings off an angel.

# CHAPTER 12

## Fall from Grace

*"I have lived on the lip of insanity, wanting to know reasons, knocking on a door. It opens. I've been knocking from the inside!"* (Rumi)

I've said it before, being a Medium is no guarantee of a peaceful life. Sophie had gone. I nose-dived.

*My energy levels hit the forest floor and a strong wind buried me in falling leaves.*

I knew I was going to struggle. I also knew, because it happened every time, that I would come through this experience with more understanding. This joining of minds and souls with my sister had almost broken me and I know she must have felt the same, although it had been her transformation more than mine and I was still carrying the burden of that responsibility. It whispered to me in the night:

*'However she is now, is your doing. She's changed forever and you're not there to see it through. You could have said 'let's agree to disagree'. You could have pointed out that you have the same core belief in helping people, so what did some disagreement matter?'*

I could have, but I hadn't. 'Why?' I asked. Then, after many such tormented nights and in the light of one glorious day, I finally stopped wondering if I had been serving my ego, rather than preserving truth, and found my sincerity in the cupboard under the stairs. I was throwing everything out looking for a box of childhood photographs. I was trying desperately to stop the thoughts in my head with this activity, but it was like trying to stop a torrent by looking sternly up at the sky. It was hopeless, I decided. I stopped looking and sat back on my heels. As I did so, I knocked a box and a picture fell onto the floor. It was a photograph of me in my school uniform and it suddenly struck me…

I put everything back neatly, calmly, reassuringly, realising that the reason I had believed everything I had told my sister was because there had been no red traffic light. With something as important as another's wellbeing, *he* would have intervened.

It was this thought that allowed me to finally try to get on with my everyday life and this little try was enough for husband, David, to ask:

"Are you back with us now?"

Always there – a priest of a man.

To keep Sophie there too, I filled part of the void that she had left by writing letters and making tapes to send to her. The tapes were filled with pieces of music that had a spiritual message. On hearing them, few people would find anything of interest, but to Sophie and me, they meant everything; they were the things we had experienced, or felt, or words that our Guides had spoken. None of the material was immediately identifiable as spiritual, or even esoteric. I even went out and bought a record by the Four Tops, because it had a few words in it that spoke for me – 'Reach Out I'll Be There'.

All of these simple synchronicities can pass us by in everyday life, but they have messages for us – just turn on the radio, and you find you're listening to the song that was going round in your head, or feel sad and find yourself tuning in to something uplifting, it's all there. It's a secret code that people deem 'coincidence', but Sophie and I had understood its worth and made it palpable. So, while our husbands and children heard nothing, we would be smiling at each other across thousands of miles. This intimacy was one of the reasons I so loved making the tapes, but I also hated receiving them. I know this sounds strange, but they pulled at my heartstrings for what I had lost. When you're a Medium, you feel *everything, everywhere* and *all at once.*

Still looking for ways to fill the void in my heart, I took up the pen. Hardly need to say it, but me being me, I went all-in, so that, by the end of the month, I was writing for at least a quarter of my day. I wasn't writing from my own head of course, I was linking into Spirit and putting their thoughts on paper. This automatic writing took over my life. I let it, of course I did, because I was trying to replace the soul connection I had experienced with Sophie and no-one could fill this, but Spirit. They had been with Sophie and me for three months and it was so delicious that I wouldn't let go. I couldn't see why it couldn't just go on.

It couldn't of course, because I'm on earth to experience life in my way. If I had been told what to do throughout my life by Spirit, what would have been the point of living? I would have learned nothing about earthly Phyllis, strengths and weakness in physical form. Such a distinct existence informed by flesh and blood like no other – the body has its own demands and the mind must battle with its needs, learn to caution it against living in the past and about wanting to survive the future, no matter what.

The demands on my body were immense – imagine, what energy this communication between worlds demands from both parties? The end result of all this for me was mental exhaustion. I sank into depression; a good, solid bout of crystallised inner struggle. The more depressed I became, the more I sat and scribbled away, burying myself in this other world; one that took me away from loss, from hurt, from every day, mundane life. It was only this activity of writing that could elevate me from my depression; this continuous, tangible link with Spirit gave me self-reliance, a sense of worth, a reason for living.

In the end, the ferocity of my writing, the intensity of my concentration, threatened to break my bonds with this world. I did actually think I was going mad at one point. Most definitely, if I'd visited a psychiatrist at this point, I'm pretty sure she or he would have diagnosed a psychiatric condition – 'talking to dead people is it? For three months now? Classic psychosis.'

I was asking constantly, "tell me what to do.  Tell me what to do…"

There was only silence in response to my questioning. I suppose the situation had become something like a child asking you to keep tying their shoelaces, just in case they make a mistake; just in case they trip and fall. Eventually you'd say, 'now you have a go'. If they kept saying they couldn't manage alone, you would stand back, urge and watch. That's just what Blue Feather did, took a step back from me, because he knew I wasn't listening.

It was at my lowest point that I finally realised the written messages I was receiving had lost the love, which is the signature of my Guide. I don't know who was feeding me with this writing at the end, but it wasn't Blue Feather. Higher spiritual messages are given with pure understanding, which is love. This communication lacked that, it contained judgments. Blue Feather had never judged me (because he believes in free will, as do all of the greater spirits), but then there are others…

… had I forgotten all that I'd learned? Had I forgotten my time in the nursing home, watching the ones that had discarded their traumatised minds to step away from this life? Had I forgotten too that, when we pass to Spirit, we remain the same personalities – we may briefly become angels in the spark of light that leaves our bodies, but we don't become angels overnight, or over death. I had lost sight of this, as I'd been in the arms of this gentle Guide for so long, allowed to be willful, to exercise my right to be wrong, and now? It just seemed that he had deserted me.

The reality was, in my obsession, I'd left my mind's door wide open and, like life, unless a friend pops by to tell you you've left your door unlocked, anyone can come in. Whoever it was communicating with me, 'he' wasn't pleasant. All of us have these dark corners of our minds (the dark spirit) and it is up to each and every one of us to recognise that element in us and to be aware that it can relate to the dark side in others and allow like minds to blend.

Normally, when you do this work, friends in Spirit are in complete control and they act like safety latches, but Blue Feather had no choice but to stand back, because if I hadn't stopped writing at this pace, he would have had to carry my burden for the rest of my life. He needed me to be me and assert myself again. He needed the old Phyllis to work with.

In order for this to happen, I had to get really angry, and I did. In a major tantrum, I threw all my writing in the dustbin, banged the lid, and banged the lid on Spirit as well. (Half-an-hour later, I crept back to the dustbin and gathered up the whole soggy, sticky mess and wept).

The next thing I did was go to a Spiritualist Church and ask for help – they told me to go away and come back next week! *Yes, I know…*

My first reaction was one of utter disbelief, then despair. Until, that is, I realised they were 'under orders', so to speak. It really was no good me going to someone else for help; that was the trouble. As a Medium, you have to be a strong energy, a powerful conductor standing between worlds. Besides, I had never given myself over to other people, ever. My character was such that I could ask for help, yes, but I'm blowed if I ever really went along with it! I had always been independent, outspoken, resilient, and Spirit wanted me back that way. It was me. It was a strong working relationship that was needed and there's one thing Spirit can see, far better than we can, and that's people pretending to be something they're not.

Despite a measure of insight at this point, I, ultimately, remained undaunted and trotted off to the local Church of England on a Sunday afternoon. The door was locked. No one home. *'Prophetic'*, I thought. There I sat that Sunday afternoon, watching the grass grow around the graves, silently, at my wit's end, alone in this world and the next, with tears blurring my vision. One last try, I took out my pen and notepad and there appeared, without hesitation:

THIS IS NOT OUR WAY IS IT?

I was too emotionally exhausted to cry anymore, too empty, too despairing. If anyone had come along at that moment and given me hope; an explanation for the seeming betrayal I felt – be it Jehovah's Witnesses, Born Again Christians, Moslems, Buddhists – I would have believed them for the rest of my days. British Gas could have converted me! Yet, here I was, bereft of all hope, and all Blue Feather could say is, 'this is not our way is it.' I knew it wasn't a question.

It got worse. You would think a person who had experienced such angelic connection in this world would have a little more faith. Unfortunately, I still had that character – I just wasn't capable of ploughing a little land carefully, so as to produce a healthy, vibrant crop. No, I had to go all-in and plough the whole dam lot, no matter how much mud got churned up in the process.

I started to write again. When I'd finished, the words stared back at me. The words told me to write to my sister and apologise for everything I had said while she was here.

*No, this was not Blue Feather.*

Above all else, above my very life, I had believed everything I had said to Sophie. Therefore, if that were my choice – if I had to write to her and denounce it all, then it was goodbye to God and to Spirit. I would not speak about it, or discuss it with anyone. I AM ME!

*Welcome back Phyllis.*

Spirit had given me the one instruction that brought me to my senses. It caused me to re-evaluate everything. That day, that, otherwise uneventful, Sunday afternoon, from out of the pyre of non-existence, Phyllis rose and listened to her higher self. I would never again allow anyone to use me from Spirit unless I chose them. From that day on, I avowed to stand on my own two feet. I had become an immense strain on my Guide and myself. Blue Feather would not have to carry my burden any more.

I had walked a tightrope between worlds, stumbled hard, teetered on the brink, but he had gently brought me back. He knew I had too much pride and he knew how to use it. He knew too that I was in danger of leaving my mind, until I was faced with denying the very beliefs that had been with me forever; everything they had told me to date. Blue Feather also knew that, even though I denounced him, I would be back. I had received too much loving proof to ignore him for too long; some evidence so significant that it had taken my breath away. These memories were to be my safety net.

My return had taken too long though and so my physical and emotional 'absences' had been noticed by others. I was to find out then how deeply worried friends and family had been about me. In David's words, as a trained psychiatric nurse, but without his professional hat on, he thought I had been 'going round the twist'. In addition, two dear friends of ours had serious concerns for me too, so they'd kept a knowing eye on me – popping in at regular intervals to assess the prevailing mood, not saying very much, but just being around. One Saturday morning though, friend Sue put her head round my back door and said:

"I know you won't want to hear this, but I ordered this audio tape 12 months ago and, bizarrely, it only arrived this morning. I'd forgotten all about it, but I think you ought to listen to it."

I glared at her.

*'Hadn't I said I wasn't discussing it with anyone!'*

I took the tape, none too graciously, and I did just play it briefly, begrudgingly, so I could say I had listened to it. A little later in the week though, I had a more kindly thought: *'I will just listen to it properly then I can be honest about it.'*

After all the seeking for help, knocking on locked doors, pushing at unyielding hearts, I found the answers I'd been seeking. All the distinct questions I'd been asking Spirit in my despair; all the things I'd been through, were answered on this one, insignificant tape. So insignificant, I can't even remember what it was called, all I knew was, it was calling me back to work for Spirit. I've said it before – there are signs all around you, if you are just prepared to be receptive and not as stubborn as me, you will see them.

Within 12 hours, the phone rang and I was asked to perform mediumship at a local Spiritualist event, as the Medium for the night had been taken ill. *'Oh how coincidental.'* I hadn't practised in public since the days of Mrs. Charge, but there it was. Why now? Because it was right and when you trust; when you can stop that mind wanting what it wants, things happen very quickly.

Now I can reflect on it, I have no way of knowing (as yet) whether I alighted from this dark night of the soul in the way that my higher self would have wished. I know I didn't emerge graciously, but I survived and I'm glad it happened because I'm not afraid of anyone or anything, here or above…

*'… but I pray that I never go through that again…'*

A few weeks later, I was no longer writing to my sister, lacking discipline or, more likely, fearing a repeat of my obsessive behaviour. I fell silent. Sophie then wrote to say she didn't want anything more to do with the family. Sounds harsh, but I hadn't explained myself and she had felt the pain of my wordless rejection and my absence; so easy to fill silences with the content of our own heads.  What was actually in my head was relief and I understood entirely.  My heart lightened. I could cope. So often our world sees parting as wrong. Why? Perhaps because few really believe that consciousness continues beyond death, or that forgiveness will wait for you there. I didn't have those reservations. I felt relief. She'd freed me from any guilt, from all responsibility and I gave thanks, and I let her go. In truth, there could be no return journey for us, no half measures – what could we possibly say to each other after this experience? Across the miles, we had sought each other, trying to remain connected, but there was too much pain in the listening, in the reading of each other's lives at such a distance. So, we let go in order to grow in our own ways and, truly, the greatest single act of love one person can offer another is to set them free. Sophie was now at liberty to live her life, her way, in Australia, with her new baby boy, Matthew, serving her churches as she saw fit. We owed each other our freedom, and we did it in our way, Sophie with undeniable finality, me, with a cowardly silence filled with all my love and gratitude because I so wanted to be free…

… free to work for Spirit.

# CHAPTER 13

## The Prophecy

*"Only a life lived for others is a life worthwhile."* (Einstein)

After the call to work again, I never stopped and 1986 was not only the year I really started to work for Spirit in earnest, but in the open too. It was 14 years after the birth of my son, Pat. Although my first appearance in public had been received well enough after my 'fall from grace', it had been a long time since I'd formally practised clairvoyance and so I felt in need of like minds and space to experiment.

This led me to enrol in a mediumship development circle in Wolverhampton, with a kindly woman called Sheila Grey. She was a very experienced Medium and teacher whose gentle command of her circle members made me think I'd like one of my own one day. I used her guidance to hone my spiritual gifts and to develop alongside kindred spirits.

It was here that, for the first time, I had the experience of someone, other than Mrs. Charge, seeing my Guide. Sheila had given us the task of addressing the circle members with a 'little talk'. I can't remember what mine was about, because unless someone writes my words down, the information just seems to flow in and out of my brain on its way to my mouth. When I'd finished, a young girl said:

"While you were standing there talking, I saw this big American Indian come and stand by you, it was amazing."

I was thrilled, even Medium's enjoy receiving messages, particularly ones like this. I wish it happened more often. It's rare, possibly because people think Mediums don't need them. Rare too, because we are just not sufficiently spiritually developed and we're also far too busy getting on with everyday life to look with a quiet mind at the world. It seems to be only when we're sitting peacefully, particularly in churches or meditating, that we perceive things not of this world.

For this reason, Sheila always impressed upon us the need to have quiet times in our lives when we could meditate. I decided to commit to practising this, although the one and only time I seemed to be able to do this, without Mrs. Charge, was when I was in bed at night, so that's when I meditated. Even though I had been an unwitting Medium since childhood, I often had great difficulty in meditating and, as you will know if you've tried it, thoughts just keep popping in and interfering with the whole process. I'd be lying in bed trying to focus on the now, when I'd suddenly remember I hadn't put any pickle in Helene's lunchbox, or put a note out for the milkman, or put the rubbish out. This type of unwelcome interference went on for three weeks and I was getting nowhere, fast.

However, in the fourth week, I was snuggled up, relaxing, ready for the mind to, hopefully, pop off into space, when a familiar voice in my head said:

"Go and sit on the bench."

*'What on earth was Blue Feather talking about?'*

The only thing I could think of was a bench that David and I used to sit on when the children were small in a grand estate called Hanbury Hall. I knew Blue Feather was trying to help, so I pictured it in my mind and suddenly recalled the feeling I'd had there, when I'd been sitting quietly watching David play with the children and I'd thought, *'what a beautiful place this is, so peaceful.'*

No sooner had this thought registered, when I was transported to the bench. It didn't even occur to me that my body was still in bed, I was just there. Quite suddenly, I was aware of someone sitting at the side of me and I thought, *'this is it! I'm going to see a spirit in his, or her, full glory!'*

Instead, I saw an old pair of shoes and, as I looked upward, I got the whole picture of a really shabby individual. It was a tramp.

*'Great! Everyone else gets angels, I get a tramp!'*

Just as I got to inspecting him more fully, a mist began to roll across his face. It occurred to me that it was a 'mask of serenity' that shrouded his features so well from my eyes. At the same time, I knew this mask was there to focus my attention on the 'main event' and I was not to bother about who he was, but rather what he wanted me to witness. The old adage about not 'judging a book by its cover' also sprang to mind and, if you believe that visions, like dreams, sometimes have meaning beyond a decluttering of the daytime mind, then a tramp is someone who has a bad reputation, and hanging out with them might just make you unpopular. There was a message for me there for sure.

We didn't speak as such, but he impressed upon me the thought that I had to look out to my side where there was a church building. It struck me then that this message was being delivered in quite a different way to Blue Feather's communications. In meditation, you get metaphor or allegory, the language of the sub-conscious mind, but when you work as a Medium, it's very different – your mind is not in control. If it is, you fail and your mind will start making things up for you because that's what it does. It doesn't like blank spaces. In meditation, it feels like there's a sense of agency, which is missing in mediumship – your mind doesn't create the process, it processes the creation.

As I continued to look, I noticed that there was a group of Down's Syndrome children playing. Again, a thought-inspiring image for me to ponder on. I could see that they had two guardians with them who were carefully watching over them and I noticed too a little boy who was just the sort of child who was going to do exactly what he wanted. (The temperament resonated with me). This little boy had spotted the conkers on the trees and he wanted one in particular. It was just out of reach. Up he stretched.

On tiptoe, he balanced precariously, grimacing with the effort, and then that look appeared on his face – the one children have just before they're going to have a tantrum. Luckily, a little girl in the group saw it and she wandered over to him and said:

"You can't have it, because it's out of reach."

So simple! It felt like another message for me, but what did this all mean? I have a tramp as a friend, so I'm probably going to attract prejudice in relation to something? I was also seeing children with developmental issues; children who were generally viewed as not expressing their full potential – was I not fulfilling mine?

I let the thoughts roll over me like the mist, as I knew the correct interpretation would settle, and I went on watching the little boy. He wasn't to be placated. He'd decided to have a tantrum anyway. One of the guardians noticed what was going on amongst the trees and she decided to try and divert the little boy:

"It's tea-time!" she exclaimed with uncompromising enthusiasm, "let's go to the café and have a cup of tea and a scone, shall we?"

That seemed to work and off they went. I counted them – 11 children and 2 guardians. The number 11 resonated with me as being associated with intuition and insight. I pondered these meanings, as I went on watching and, without moving, I could see them inside the café.

I listened, as one of the guardians ordered cream teas. I heard the waitress say:

"We haven't got any more."

That was just too much for the little boy and his face crumpled, ready for a spectacular tantrum. Again, one of the guardians intervened:

"Rather than scones, why don't we have – by far and away – the best cake ever!"

The little boy didn't look too convinced, but was soon distracted by the other children's glee. He joined in, clasping his hands together. In turn, my attention withdrew and I was, again, aware of the tramp next to me. Now, I was impressed with the thought:

*'Seems we would sometimes have to eat cake…'*

The moral? I translated it as, simply, we don't always get what we want and, maybe, that's because we can do even better? Then the tramp drew my attention back and he indicated that I should watch in front of me and see what came through the fields. I looked, there came a dark grey mist and it got thicker and, when it reached us, it swallowed us whole. I felt a little apprehensive, but the thought came to me: *'well, if he's here, I will be ok; otherwise he'd have moved me out of danger.'*

I looked at him for reassurance, but he wasn't there, just dark grey mist which started to lift and grow lighter and then I saw what I first thought was a rope. It came farther forward until I could see that it was wider, more solid. It was actually a pillar, ornately twisted. As if in recognition of that thought, it grew in stature before my very eyes and, as I looked up to the top of it, I could see that it was holding up a church ceiling.

Now I realised this was a prophecy – I believed it meant I was to set up a church. This church wasn't going to be ornate, or traditional, but it would make my abilities and my spiritual views public for the first time, beyond the confines of closeted Spiritualist meetings and a few close friends. This meant that I would not be able to hide my gift in the mist. It would be in full sight and I would be vulnerable to the prejudice I feared; people would see me as undesirable, just like the tramp.

It would be a time when, like the little boy, I was to be disappointed somehow; a time when I would not receive what I wanted, but what everyone else needed. It would be a place where people could reach their full spiritual potential without judgement, or fear of prejudice. This meant I would have to be as strong as the ornate pillar I'd just seen; one that was holding up the church. It represented a column of spiritual strength; a conduit through which the knowledge would flow. It was a support and a connection that I would have to learn to build in the years to come.

Not only this, but if I wanted the church to have real value, it would need a strong connection with Spirit, I would have to fill it with those who could deliver mediumship of strength, of quality, deliver messages that would stand the test of time. I would need to teach them myself, as Mrs. Charge had taught me.

Suddenly, I was back in bed, thinking, *'that was great!'* I couldn't wait for the next night, to return, to be totally engrossed in a world of prophecy and to be shown the way more clearly. Didn't happen … probably because the message had been firmly and memorably sent and it had been an important one – a spiritual goal for me – and so it had to stand alone if it were to stand the test of time.

And stand the test of time it did. It was to be several years after this that I was sitting in a church, as a spectator, and watching a Medium at work. She was a movable object, bending to the will of the person in the audience who was saying, "I don't understand that name, I do remember a Bill though." The Medium would then obligingly continue her message about someone called 'Bill'.

I thought, *'for goodness sake, stick to your guns'* and *'don't mess about'; 'don't you know?'*

Ultimately, I thought, *'I could teach you to do better than that.'* Isn't it true that the real teachers in our world are often those we criticise? Stupid, because while we find fault in everyone else, we don't listen to ourselves – she was calling me to teach her. She was reminding me of my spiritual goal, delivered in a meditation years before. She was reminding me that Spirit needed good Mediums; ones who would 'say it as it's given'; otherwise what is the point?

Strong Mediums have their heads in a cloud – an energy cloud – when they work. When I work in public, I spend a few minutes before the service to shut out the external world and 'be' in this energy and this is what being in a mediumship development circle should teach – how to recognise that energy and use it.

*Cue Phyllis.*

I kept these thoughts to myself, but I detected two people there who I 'knew' were on the same wavelength and they were to become firm friends – Rose and Sandra. At the time, I didn't wonder if they were the two guardians in my vision, but they *were* instrumental in building the column that would support my spiritual goal and, as we grew to know each other, we began to talk about starting a developmental circle of our own. And then, very quickly, another two kindred spirits came along – a woman called Melinda and another called Yvonne. Now, I had enough friends about me to support me. Melinda, in particular, was a guiding force and, very quietly (as is often the case), she gently guided the circle into reality. Melinda had a solid character; just the sort of person to motivate you into doing something about your dreams.

My first circle ran successfully for 12 months and I learned a lot. I used all the skills I'd acquired from running Weightwatchers, but instead of motivating them to lose their bodies, I was teaching them to 'lose their minds' instead.

I know I didn't always get it right, when my ego took over, but I didn't stop trying. Often, I would want to push individuals a little harder than they wanted, knowing deep down that whilst they had little faith in their abilities, they really were capable of doing the things I was asking of them and, sometimes, I had to learn to put the damper on a lively spirit, whose imagination was working overtime! It was my training ground – people came and went until a core remained, upon whom I could rely to do the real work. Others left because they had just wanted messages for themselves – at their core was selfishness and it wouldn't support anything but itself.

Throughout this, I gradually learned to stand alone, as many teachers do. Indeed, one day, you wake up and it seems you have left everyone behind; you're just sitting on the bench, feeling a little vulnerable and wondering what people think of you. You end up feeling at a distance from them – in their minds, not yours – and so you end up alone.

I was alone in witnessing how people could be so totally unaware of when and how Spirit were working with them, or me for that matter – they did not seem aware of when my Guide would speak. In fact, I was forever being amazed that people just didn't seem to realise that such wisdom could not be coming from a housewife called Phyllis. At these times, I was very much aware of my ego, I wanted to believe it was me.

Such grandiose feelings don't last long when you're working with Spirit though and I might have thought I was doing well until, one night, I turned up for circle with Yvonne, only to find we were the only ones there – where had everyone gone? The next Monday, it was just Yvonne, Sandra, Rose and Melinda (my friends).

Painful, but purposeful as, when we chatted that evening, my night-time meditation came back to me quite clearly and I told my friends about a church that would one day be built. We played with the idea, what would we do, where would it be, who would do what? The seeds were sown, but for now life intervened – Yvonne bought a shop, I moved to Droitwich, Sandra became extra busy with work, and so on. However, while that faded back into the mist for now, it wasn't long before Sandra and myself were being pestered to start a circle in Droitwich. There was no church here either and so there were people who were not able to fulfil their spiritual potential; they wanted somewhere to meet with like minds.

We set up another circle. At the time, I didn't wonder if this were the bit in my vision about going where I was needed, not getting what I wanted, but then, one night, I decided to split the 11 members up into small groups to practise clairvoyance. I told them to take themselves out of the circle to work in private with their group member and to give each other clairvoyance for 15 minutes. After which, we were to reform the circle and I would interpret, where necessary, any images and thoughts they had received.

One of the pairs (a woman called Pam and a man called Jack) had been engrossed in their discussions and when I asked them to share their experiences, far from describing their feelings, thoughts and senses, and without a word from me, they said:

"What about a church in Droitwich?"

*'Keep quiet, Phyllis, wait and see what's coming next…'* Could it be the 'guardians' had spoken and now the metaphorical children were to be organised?

Slowly, other circle members began to join in and they were becoming enthusiastic about the idea, but would there be enough people ready to step up? Starting a church takes a lot of time and effort, it has to be well thought out and no-one gets paid. It's not to be undertaken lightly. Were we going to find suitable people to fulfil the roles we needed? We needed people who weren't afraid to address an audience (to chair for the Medium); we needed someone to book Mediums, compose letters, write adverts, keep a calendar, and act as Treasurer for its upkeep. Who would be willing to make tea, bake cakes, wash up, put out chairs, and clean up afterwards? Then there was the issue of where we could actually locate this church, and how much would it cost?

No-one makes money from these ventures because of the very nature of the underlying principles. They are just places where people of like minds can safely gather and be accepted; be free to explore their own beliefs without prejudice, but they can't be run on fresh air. Were people going to be generous enough to invest their time, money and effort in such a venture?

On and on the discussions went. Round and round in my head the questions circled, yet I knew that, if it were something Spirit valued, it would get done.

And it did.

Most of it seemed to happen around me, unperceptively, swirling around in the mist and occasionally surfacing for me to see. When the church opened its doors in January 1990, on an inauspicious Tuesday night, so many people came that we had to hunt around for chairs. It was nerve-racking and yet exhilarating, particularly as people who had set up churches miles away came to support us on this our first night. The Church (called the 'Blue Lodge'[1]) still runs

---

[1] *The Blue Lodge*, Droitwich Spiritual Centre, The Barn, New Chawson Lane, Droitwich. WR9 0AQ. GB.

on a Tuesday night and it will go on until it's no longer needed.

That first night, I remember a very simple message that I gave a young girl. I remember it because, to me, it exemplifies how I work and what I'm about as a Natural Medium, even in churches. As I scanned the audience, looking for where to start, I came across a mum and daughter sitting together. The Mum was saying, over and over in her head, *'tell her to stop worrying about her weight'.* I knew it would cause embarrassment to give that message to a young girl in front of a lot of people, so I waited till afterwards and then I told her:

"I have a man here who is telling me to tell you that you should stop worrying about your weight."

She gasped – it obviously meant something to her. She told me, "that's my Dad. He was always saying that to me."

This simple message told her that he still worried about her. Nothing else needed to be said, as she was far more likely to listen to him than anyone else, particularly her mother. There were no fanfares, no bright lights, just genuine, helpful communication, designed to improve the lives of those on earth.

All the good fortune, and the ease with which that first night happened, was a spiritual experience with a lot of hard work from Guides and helpers. If people would listen to their own helpers (or listen to their inspiration if you prefer), then there would never be any disagreements when it came to such communal ventures, for these are very much in the hands of Spirit, they are not ours to dominate. Spirit never gets a word of thanks for their help and support of course, they just get to listen to us worrying, or arguing, over life's little problems.

Since then, there have been a thousand messages given to people, a thousand allegories and prophecies from Spirit, a thousand translations. My work for Spirit culminated in this – the development of a local church and a circle to 'grow' Mediums to serve it. From my point of view then, there is little more to be said, for it was the pinnacle of my spiritual life.

Mrs. Charge and Phyllis
(aged 20. Whitsun 1966)

# CHAPTER 14

## Between Worlds

*"All the darkness in the world cannot extinguish the light of a single candle."* (St. Francis of Assisi)

After the church had been set up, the Gulf War started and my life got even busier transitioning souls to spirit. Throughout this war, I spent my last hour, before the family got home, to sit and link into spirit, and to help soldiers and civilians alike pass over. Sometimes, this was intense, more so when there was a mass loss of life – so many people and what you see in your head has no national boundaries – death strips away such identity and all souls pass. For many people, it is the first time they 'see' who they really are and, with all the social conventions stripped away, there is just a spiritual being. We all have to ask ourselves, *will it be enough?*

My role in this work is to be a living bridge between worlds, I have a familiar, human energy; I am easily recognisable and I help whoever I am directed to, whether they be civilians, children, or soldiers on both sides and sometimes even the animals that were with them. You help whoever you can. There is no judgment and when there are a lot of souls to go at one time, it takes immense focus, resilience and co-operation with Guides and helpers.

Despite all the shared, positive energy and co-operation, I found working to transition souls in the Gulf War harder than the Falklands War before it. I think this was because the extensive televised coverage just kept reminding me of what I'd seen in my head. It also vividly revived those memories I had of the Falklands War, specifically the shocking image of the BBC coverage of the Sir Galahad being bombed – the resultant fireball became one of the most defining images of that war and, for me, particularly traumatic because it had been bombed at the very moment I was linking in to Spirit. The fireball engulfed me. It was hard not to be part of the chaos and to catch my breath and remind myself why I was there. It was then difficult to avoid being exposed to it time and time again in the BBC's repeats of the event.

Transitioning a soul can be particularly hard when there is disbelief on top of a 'fighting spirit' – some are firmly in survival mode and breaking through can be tough when they die very quickly. There's no apparent time to assimilate the change. Yet it *does* happen and that's because time slows – breathes differently there – something like the experience of being in extreme danger, or a traumatic accident, when you see things in slow motion. It can be as slow as the realisation needs to be to ensure the person is not lost in the process.

Having said that, sometimes, the journey is unexpectedly easy. Some souls are just ready to go – they've felt enough pain in themselves and seen too much in others. At these times, spirits recognise you quickly and you feel them reaching out to you and you always want to hold them tight. *You become the single light in the darkness.*

This transitioning between worlds remains a very important part of my work, but very private, and it's not confined to war. In fact, usually, I work with individuals who come for a 'sitting' because they've discovered they are ill.

Recently, I had a lovely Australian lad, called Sam, arrive at my door. He literally just turned up – I suspect someone from the church told him about me – my address is really no secret. Sam had come to the UK for treatment, but now he knew he'd exhausted his options and was going home to die. Sam had a brain tumour. He was 22. He just wanted to know he'd be ok. Of course I knew he would be. My job was to make sure he knew that too.

I asked him to choose to trust me and I took him to a place in his imagination – a meadow, where there was a stream running into a river, a river that ran into the sea, and told him this would be the journey he would take. I told him that's how we pass over and into the beyond – 'it's water that gives us life on earth and it's water that will take us away.' This is why it's not unusual for people to see a stream or a lake in the course of transitioning to the spirit world. The point of this exercise was to put the image into Sam's mind, so that when he saw it again, he would feel reassured; he would know what was about to happen. It can be as easy as that.

It is so important to help souls fulfil that part of the human journey that is always missing from text books or life coaching sessions – to evidence the continuation of life and to assist with that final journey from this world to the next. For that reason, I know that when I'm too old to teach aspiring Mediums or serve churches, this is something I will never stop doing.

### The River Cannot Go Back

(this excerpt is credited to
Kahlil Gibran)

*"The river can not go back.*
*Nobody can go back.*
*To go back is impossible in existence.*
*The river needs to take the risk of entering the ocean*
*because only then will fear disappear,*
*because that's where the river will know*
*it's not about disappearing into the ocean,*
*but of becoming the ocean."*

# CHAPTER 15

## The Day After

*"What is a day to an immortal soul! A breath,
no more."* (Thomas Bailey Aldrich)

I've spent hours raking through the past, some of which I had been hoping to forget and now I'm trying to move on in more ways than one – move on from reliving the past and move on from the Gulf War. The war had taken its toll on me and the incongruity of transitioning souls in the context of everyday life only becomes clear when it's viewed against the backdrop of a normal, family day. So, I decided that, today, would be the last day of the book and I would tell you about my day.

Today is another fairly normal one for me. David left the house this morning in a hurry, like a whirlwind looking for something to demolish with a piece of toast in his mouth and a few comforting words, which could have been, 'I love you dearest wife, my reason for living, my desert rose…' Except it wasn't. I just used poetic licence because he had his mouth full of love for me.

David will always keep my feet on the ground. He's a great leveller. Even after a spectacular clairvoyance session, I'm quickly brought back down to earth when he asks, 'what's for tea?' I'm soon back to thinking about the washing, the lunches and the shopping lists with David.

As for son, Pat – who now works in a landscape gardening and maintenance firm – he left quietly on his bike this morning as usual, with his sandwiches tucked into his saddlebag. You know, I often get the impression with Pat that he doesn't feel as though he's achieved anything in life, but on a spiritual level, he's achieved everything – he gives love freely and asks for no reward. If a mother can look to her son for an example, then I would want to be as kind as he.

Helene has gone off to 'the office' where she started humbly as a junior. I was going to say 'quietly', but she's just the opposite of Pat – a free spirit and a law unto herself. (I can't say I wonder where she got that from). She never asks anybody to do anything that she wouldn't do herself, always striving to be as good as she can, but she has to experiment with everything along her way. No angel, my Helene, but she's working on it.

As for me, I've just loaded the week's washing and Hilary and I are listening to it chugging through its routine with all the decorum of a rock band in a monastery, as I reflect on the fact that I'm feeling a little empty.

I finished work early in my own little curtain studio. I worked all day Sunday, just so I could have half-a-day off today to sit and talk to Hilary. My work is still an outlet for my creativity, working with the colours that I've always loved and it gives me the freedom and the money to do my spirit work.

Most weeks, I practise mediumship in formal surroundings, at pre-arranged times and, not only at the local church I witnessed being built from the ground up in Droitwich, but at other churches around the country. In fact, I serve around 68 churches and I normally do so on Wednesday and Sunday evenings.

At such times, and as weary as I may become, I never grow tired of watching stranger's faces when they find out where I'm coming from; who I am, when they discover that I haven't got two heads and I'm not carrying a folding broomstick in my handbag. I'm still always intrigued when Spirit join in with my everyday conversations too and people just don't realise what's happening.

After this type of work, I really love to sit and talk with like minds – as I do on alternate Tuesday evenings with the circle members – to discuss anything and everything; to experiment – not always for Spirit messages – but just to bounce ideas round with a view to creating enough freedom to expand consciousness. Spirit need people to work with and it starts with de-limiting human consciousness and this is the function of the development circle I run – it is a very important part of my work to allow the spirit of those in this world and the next to commune.

In fact, although setting up the local circle and church felt like the culmination of my life, I have always had a dream of setting up a centre where people could come and talk, to discuss and experiment with their life force; their own spiritual awareness and awakening.

I have no other ambitions in life other than this now, apart from seeing the happiness of my own family; my hope is for them to blossom. That hope isn't restricted to my own nearest and dearest, but extends to the greater family of mankind – not only in this world, but in the spirit world too.

I've found something out about myself recently too. I've discovered that I need a great deal of peace; time when I'm not with anyone, time to recover strength. I've found that the more spirit work I do, the more peace time I need in order to find my balance again. If I don't get that balance right, I can easily become depressed. Sometimes, it's a constant battle to stay optimistic about life and that's an ongoing problem for me. Being a Medium is no guarantee of a happy life, that's for sure.

I have strong views too, as you will probably know by now. I now hate negative prejudice in any shape or form. I have no racial prejudice, so far as I am aware. I am appalled by any restriction on people's freedom to choose their own religions, or ways of being, and I take great pains in dealing with people who aren't the accepted 'norm', or just those who are different. I like people to be different, to be unique – their minds are in a healthy place.

Later, I look forward to retirement, when I can dedicate my time to spiritual unfoldment; to be able to move in harmony with everything around me, with no routines. I wouldn't mind cleaning the house still and making a home, but I'd want to go out when I wanted, to have no responsibilities, just peace.

And then, around this time, shall come death. Fortunately, I had a vision in my 20s, and, whilst I admit I don't understand all of it (yet), the gist of it was that I went out of a little house, along the side of it and through an archway into the garden and there, standing amongst flowers of every size and colour (but particularly roses), was a man dressed in a simple, white garment. As I approach, he holds out his arms to me and says, 'come with me, it's time to take you to a new home'. I don't know who he is yet.

Very simply, when I see that man again, I will know it's time for me to go, but I'm thrilled to see I will still have the use of my legs and I will be walking into Spirit. I would want to leave you with the same thought – start to walk towards your God (whatever form that takes) and see who comes to help you along the way.

I will end, if I may, by introducing you properly to those who have been helping me along my way.

## Farewell from my Guide and Helpers

Thank you my Guide and helpers for making this book possible. It is only right that I should end by introducing you to the world.

My Guide, Blue Feather, has never been very far away, even when I thought he had deserted me, this is because he was (is) my friend in this life. Although he finally, formally, introduced himself those many years ago in America, with the majesty of an American Indian, he would tell you that this incarnation was a long time ago and he rarely aligns himself to a particular human group these days. He's my personal guide, gatekeeper, conductor, chairman and I sometimes call him 'His Lordship' when I think he's not listening. He will always be the first and last, yet, the more I work, the more I become conscious of my other helpers and they change depending on the task needed. Just like us they have skills in different areas. Let me introduce them to you.

**Salamander** – my relationship with this entity is not what I would call a loving one in that he wouldn't just pop in for a chat. No, I become aware of him when great strength is needed. For instance, when there are critics in the audience. I remember one occasion, when I was just 17, working under Mrs. Charge, when I was giving an address in church and a man in the audience started to interrupt, none too politely. I offered up my thoughts, *'help me'*, I asked.

Whoosh! Without missing a beat (people told me afterwards), I began to tell this man that he 'was a child in his God's eyes and, as such, was afforded all the respect of a child, but no more…' There had been more, but it flowed through and cannot be recalled now. That man became very quiet indeed.

I learned later that there were a lot of converts to the belief in the existence of a spirit world that evening, as even the hardest critic was content to listen to a naïve 17-year old commanding their attention. They were spell-bound.

In adulthood, this channelling happened a few times, but one that springs to mind was when, mid-speech, a man walked from the back of the church to come and stand right in front of my face and tell me what a charlatan I was. I don't know what had happened to make him feel so much passion, but Salamander launched into a sermon (not an attack I must say) that caused the man to turn on his heels and leave the church.

That's Salamander – strong and trustworthy, rock-solid, not hard though. I lean on him when necessary, so our relationship is more a teacher-pupil one.

**Tamari** – (This name is the closest interpretation I can achieve).  In time, I learned that he was actually from southern Kenya, a member of the Maasai. Tamari is friendlier than Salamander, yet more powerful than both Salamander and Blue Feather put together when it comes to healing, and he will even follow up healing on his own behalf. If he recognises someone is unwell in my company, he will estrange himself from me and go and give healing to them for as long as necessary. We are very much part of each other, Tamari and I. He is absolutely reliable when it comes to 'atmosphere'. Sometimes, when you work in different buildings, as I do, a certain feeling or atmosphere can be present. When it is not a helpful one, then Tamari is there to change it into positive energy.

On occasions, he has even warned me not to do something. One circle night, he informed me there was a troublesome influence going to be there and, as my energy was depleted, he felt it wise that I stay away. I told a friend of mine, called Chris (also a Medium) and she kindly volunteered to take my place. She told me afterwards that it was 'a good job' I hadn't gone because I would have walked into an ambush from a small faction. Unfortunately, human competition isn't confined to offices and politics. As she was fore-warned though, she was able to put a stop to it immediately.

Similarly, when I'm about to give a private sitting to someone and Tamari comes into the room, then I know I'm in for a hard time. This is because he has a real skill in calming people who need to accept what has to be said, even when they're very difficult. He is also good with nervous people. To sum him up, given the power of his healing, if he asked me to walk through the 'gates of hell' with him to help a lost soul, I would go.

**Chan** – I was with Mrs. Charge when I became conscious of him and his Chinese philosophy of 'wu wei'. This concept emphasises taking action when necessary, but not using excessive effort, which tends to introduce tension into the mix. It's the Western world's version of 'walking in faith' I guess. I gave Chan the only Chinese name I knew at 16 and it stuck. At this time, he only came to introduce a young Chinese girl to me (whom I called 'Butterfly' because she was so gentle and just seemed to flit in and out).

These two – Chan and Butterfly – seem to pair up for healing purposes, but, that said and as I relate this, Chan has come strongly back into my world in his own right to talk as a teacher. As a Medium, I know that he has come to give me extra help as I walk into a new phase of my life or, in his words, 'to lighten the discovery'.

I have spoken elsewhere in the book about the novel nature of Guides and why they tend to have unusual names. It is true to say that many of the wisest Spirits are those who have transitioned the most; they are the oldest, hence the old-fashioned names. The fact that some are American Indian or Chinese is of little relevance to them, or me, suffice to say that these cultures have a greater understanding of the forces around them through their philosophies than many other civilisations and are, therefore, more adept at using the energies that this form of communication requires.

For now, dear friend, I will leave you with Chan's words – I hope my communication with you will 'lighten your discovery'.

# POSTSCRIPT

*"In the end, only three things matter; how much you loved, how gently you lived and how gracefully you let go of things not meant for you."* (Buddha)

This book took over 30 years to see the light of day after that day in 1991 and a day when the Gulf War had finally allowed Phyllis to draw breath. It took so long, not only because we went in different directions, but because our meeting got interrupted and, in my head, there were things left unsaid. In the end though, what we think is important at the time turns out to be just flotsam – as intriguing as it seems, it's still just 'stuff' floating passed us. The point really is to stay in that crystal clear, glass-bottomed boat, so you never lose sight of your true depths; the real magic guiding you.

So now as I look back, I suspect this book just took as long as it needed to, but back then in 1991 on our last visit, I hadn't been so philosophical. I remember feeling slightly annoyed when Blue Feather decided to interrupt us and I was then struggling to write quickly enough.

In hindsight, this was fortunate indeed, as it left me with little time to engage that logical mind – the one that keeps a running commentary on what is plausible and what is not. In truth, I never doubted Phyllis's integrity, but it doesn't stop you questioning, particularly when you have quite a rational mind to satisfy. Nonetheless, fairly quickly, even I began to realise that what I was writing wasn't coming from Phyllis.

I was just showing Phyllis some photographs of my life – after all, she'd shared so much of hers with me, I wanted to give something back. One in particular held her gaze. She stared at the picture while I was wittering on about my springer spaniel, Jess. There's a sharp intake of breath:

"He knows him."

"Who, Phyllis?" Phyllis indicates the man standing beside the spaniel. It's my husband.

"Blue Feather remembers this gentleman."

I was so taken aback by the idea of Blue Feather and my husband knowing each other somehow – and with all the *what!? how!? when!?* that entails – that I failed to write down much of what was said. I was thinking, 'when was this exactly? Was it in a previous incarnation? Were they both Indians, same tribe, warring factions – what?' *You get the idea.*

This cognitive dissonance was probably just as well, as my husband didn't believe in the existence of any spiritual entity and he wouldn't have appreciated being documented either. However, the description of his character was impressive to me. Blue Feather referred to him as 'a great oak who would not bend with the wind, but who would stand against it.' He added, 'in a storm it would be wise to learn to bend rather than fall to break the hearts of those around as well as its own.'

You have no idea just how on point this is.

It was at this stage – now he'd gained my attention and a deal of credibility – that he could launch into his dialogue with the knowledge that I was now actively listening as Phyllis channelled him.

## Blue Feather Speaks

*Phyllis can hold our vibration in short bursts. You will therefore experience a mixture of our thoughts interpreted by Phyllis and direct communication which may, to your ears, sometimes sound quaint. This communication is a mixture of my knowledge and intelligence combined with hers, until you cannot distinguish between the two of us. To you, it must seem as though Phyllis is simply talking naturally, but to the initiated, it would indeed appear that an exchange of thought is taking place. In this exchange, there is a loss in translation from time to time. This is the result, not only of our diverse cultures, but because many concepts have gained undue impetus in your world. Nonetheless, there is communication of virtue and value.*

*This degree of harmony arises only when you combine efforts with each other. We would ask that each of you, at some quiet time, spend a little thought on harmonising with each other, rather than judging. Offer up your own shortcomings, so that they may be filled by your brother with his strengths and, in turn, let him offer to you his weaknesses. In this way, will you learn to live and work in harmony, as do we. Such is the relationship between Medium and Guide, or there would be no communication of value.*

*We would ask you to remember that we have spent many years working with each other, harmonising, and this conversational approach suits Phyllis' personality and lifestyle, because she meets many troubled people who know little of the existence of Spirit. We therefore help them, frequently without their knowledge, through Phyllis.*

*This, our working relationship, was never meant to be emulated by anyone and you will all work in a different way, for you are all potential*

*Mediums; the potential word of Spirit and not all of you will stand on a platform to do your work. There is no right way, only a successful combination of language, personality, culture and, above all else, love. Beyond this, I would say that as the girl (Phyllis) came from an English background and I from a North American Indian one, then we have done well.*

*We would speak, specifically, of the word 'Guide' to you. Know this of your own Guide; their ability to move you is as the wind that moves softly through the trees — they can gently inspire you, but they cannot take away the life that makes you grow, nor end your life at any given time, no matter the pain. It is in the way that the sapling which, once fed by the torrent, is weakened by its kindness; it struggles to hold on to the Mother Earth, it stretches out its roots into the soil, searching for a greater understanding, until it can find peace. And when the storm has passed, the sapling, though battered, is stronger, more resilient and its gaze upon the sun is as a gift to the Great Spirit. No, it is not possible for us to stop your growth, no matter the pain.*

*Nor is it possible to feed you as the earth feeds you, but we give the food of knowledge — we are fishers of men. The Guide can take the combined wisdom of Spirit, our experiences of many lives, and scatter it on the wind that is the breath of the Great Spirit. When you, as individuals, have gathered enough knowledge to pass on to another, then you must take the responsibility that this naturally brings in catching the wind in your sails.*

*It would be a very courageous person who takes this endeavour upon themselves to change the direction of another without a great deal of thought and, even then, there will be times when this responsibility will be made apparent to you, as you relate your new-found knowledge to another human being who is not ready to accept such thoughts. They will tell you that you are wrong; that it is untrue. You now experience the tangible pain of this responsibility, as you run aground on their rejection.*

*To us, in Spirit, their, or your, rejection has no meaning, other than it is not 'right knowledge' for you now. That information will, one day, be relevant, as no word is ever given unless it is properly meant. We take no notice of time, for it is relative only to perception and there will be a time for you when you will find that the words given were but signposts to help you along your way. If you ignore them, it is of no consequence, we do not blame you – would you blame a blind man for ignoring the light? What good does it appear to do him, he asks, failing to notice that he can now see.*

*We would ask only this – try not to judge the wisdom of the words, but hold them in your thoughts until you see them clearly as the signpost that is pointing to the pathway you must take. They are there for every individual, laid with loving care by your Guides. There is not one person, out of the millions of people who walk your earth, who do not have their signposts to help them. It may seem inconceivable to you that all people have someone at their side, but I uphold this belief with my honour. We go on because hope is ours; there is no help who does not breathe by your side with hope.*

*Can you now imagine what existence these spirit helpers have when their guidance is never recognised; when not once do you see one signpost? Unrecognised, all a helper can do is to translate negative thoughts into positive ones; in other words, to neutralise hate.*

*I would that we could offer you the formulae for the translation of energy from negative to positive, but the greatest minds of your earth are as children to our mind. You say, 'from out of the mouths of babes' will come wisdom but, with life's transitions, there comes the wisdom of the soul. It is with this depth of knowledge that we reach out to you, not with our words, but with our souls. Then shall they listen; then shall they know our mind, our science. Until then:*

> *I will follow you until the ends of time*
> *Until the fountain's last sparkling drop*
> *Until the wind's last faint whisper*
> *Until the fire's last burning ember*
> *And you shall know me at last.*

# ABOUT THE AUTHOR

Hilary Harcourt (real name, Hilary Burns) lives with her husband, two cocker spaniels and Belle, the horse, in the Forest of Dean in the UK. She has a master's degree in the Social Sciences and lectured at the Universities of Worcester, Falmouth and Exeter. She specialised in Neurodiversity. Although published in her field of expertise, this is Hilary's first publication in this genre, although her exploration of this phenomena has been a lifelong one.

Phyllis's story is to be continued in

*'Working with Angels'*

*Making Angels*

**Pre-launch Notification**

Watch out for the natural talent of

*'Steve Young Horsemanship'*

another biography by Hilary Harcourt.

Printed in Great Britain
by Amazon

27532823R00108